THE
GOSPEL IN THE OLD TESTAMENT

THE GOSPEL

IN THE

OLD TESTAMENT

BY THE REV.

C. F. BURNEY, M.A., D.Litt.

ORIEL PROFESSOR OF THE INTERPRETATION OF HOLY SCRIPTURE
AT OXFORD
FELLOW OF ORIEL AND ST. JOHN'S COLLEGES
CANON OF ROCHESTER

PUBLISHERS
Eugene, Oregon

Wipf and Stock Publishers
199 W 8th Ave, Suite 3
Eugene, OR 97401

The Gospel in the Old Testament
By Burney, C.F.
ISBN: 1-59752-114-0
Publication date 3/8/2005
Previously published by T&T Clark, 1921

PREFACE.

——◆——

IT can hardly be questioned that at present one of
the most pressing needs of religion upon the
intellectual side is the reinterpretation of the
spiritual teaching of the Old Testament, and the
bringing of that teaching into its true relation to
the Christian revelation as contained in the New
Testament. Modern critical and scientific study is
believed by many to have discredited the religious
value of the Old Testament. Numbers of people
who have but a vague and hearsay knowledge of " the
Higher Criticism " think that its aim—or, at any rate,
its result—has been to pull down and destroy rather
than to build up. Even the Christian preacher, if, as
too often is the case, he is untrained and unversed in
modern Old Testament study, is apt to regard the
Old Testament as an incubus rather than as a help to
his teaching. He avoids it in his sermons; he is
perplexed as to the sense in which divine inspiration
can be claimed for it; sometimes he frankly confesses
his desire to lay it aside altogether, and to start from
the New Testament.

Many years of critical study have convinced the
present writer that the Old Testament Scriptures

form a possession of abiding and incalculable value to Christianity. Whether we view them as the record of a long evolution "by many parts and in many manners," leading up in the fulness of time to the Gospel-revelation, or as a storehouse of spiritual teaching and aspiration which still at the present day makes its appeal to the Christian conscience, we may find in them one of the most powerful arguments for the truth of our Faith. Studied in the light of the historical circumstances which helped to shape and determine it, the religious evolution cannot otherwise be explained than as God-inspired: the Old Testament still points forward to Christ, Who draws together in His single Person its different spiritual ideals, and fulfils beyond all human expectation their highest possibilities. This fact, so far from being weakened through the minute critical study which the Old Testament has undergone, may truly be said to stand out with ever-increasing clearness.

The sermons contained in this volume aim at placing certain aspects of the religious teaching of the Old Testament in their historical setting, at showing their intimate connexion with the New Testament revelation, and at applying them practically to the religious needs of the present day. The sermons were not written with a view to publication or designed to form a single continuous series. The writer felt that the interpretation of Holy Scripture, which forms his professorial work at Oxford, ought rightly to form also the main subject of his preaching.

The events of the past six years have served to bring
into clearer relief the permanent religious value of
much of the Old Testament teaching, and many of
the sermons stand in relation to burning questions
which were directly raised by the war, and form as it
were landmarks of stages in the crisis through which
we have passed. These have been allowed to remain
as they were written, on the view that their application to the special circumstances of the moment would
illustrate the more clearly the abiding moral and
spiritual importance of the Old Testament. Their
grouping under this aspect may be gathered from the
dates which are given in the Table of Contents. As
arranged in the book they follow the natural Old
Testament order ; and it has happened, without special
design, that they offer an outline of Old Testament
history in relation to religious thought which is fairly
continuous for a considerable period.[1] Thus the writer
hopes that the book may not be without value as a
brief introduction to the historical study of Old
Testament religion.

The writer's thanks are due to the editor of the
Interpreter for permission to reprint Sermons V. and VI.

C. F. BURNEY.

THE PRECINCT,
ROCHESTER, *September* 1920.

---

[1] See, for the 9th century B.C., No. 5 ; for the earlier 8th century,
Nos. 7 and 8 ; for the later 8th century, Nos. 9 and 19 ; for the
7th century, No. 10 ; for the Exilic period, Nos. 11, 12 ; for the post-
Exilic period, No. 13.

CONTENTS.

———＋———

THE GOSPEL IN THE OLD TESTAMENT.

I.

THE EARLY NARRATIVES OF GENESIS.

"As through one man's disobedience the many were made sinners, even so through the obedience of one shall the many be made righteous."—ROM. v. 19.

AS we listened to the First Lesson for this morning's service,[1] some of us may perhaps have questioned ourselves as to whether the Church was not rather behind the times in still prescribing the public reading of the early chapters of Genesis. We may have speculated as to what can be the present-day value of these old stories from a religious point of view, now that we have come to know so much about their origin, and have found out that in many particulars they bear a close resemblance to the stories of early Babylonian mythology, which deal with the origin of the world, and the facts of its early history.

It is quite true that the outward setting of the

[1] Sexagesima Sunday : Gen. iii.

Hebrew stories of the Creation, the Flood, the diffusion
of man upon the earth, and, we may probably add,
the story of the Fall, are part of the common heritage
of Semitic mythology. These speculations appear to
have grown up in Babylonia, where civilization was
of immense antiquity, and to have been borrowed by
the Hebrews from the Babylonians, either when the
Hebrew tribes broke off from the parent-stock and
migrated westward, or at some subsequent period
when Babylonian influence made itself felt in the
lands which lay to the immediate west.

What then, apart from their antiquarian interest,
is the abiding value of these narratives ? What value
do they possess sufficient to justify the reading of them
from time to time as the first lesson in church ? Here
we open up the question of the standpoint from which
we ought to regard the Old Testament literature as
a whole ; and we must, in the first place, touch very
briefly upon this subject. The point of view which
I would suggest is in no way new-fangled or re-
volutionary, for it may claim an antiquity and an
authority as high as that of the New Testament.
When I make this claim, I am referring to the opening
words of the writer of the Epistle to the Hebrews :
" God, having of old time spoken unto the fathers in
the prophets by many portions and in many manners,
hath at the end of these days spoken unto us in His
Son." These words, I believe, cover everything which
I shall have to say to you.

In the first place, we are bound to regard the Old

Testament as containing the voice of God speaking to man. The Old Testament writers were actuated primarily, and mainly, by a *religious* purpose. If once we lose sight of this fact, and think that we are to go to the Old Testament for exact historical information, or for accurate scientific knowledge, we are certain to go wrong and to be disappointed. For it is in the sphere of *religious truth* that the inspiration of the Old Testament is found. The writing in which the truth is contained, whether it take the form of history or any other form, is merely the human framework; and, as such, subject to the limitations of human method.

And secondly, God spoke unto the fathers "by many parts"; *i.e.* the partial and fragmentary character of the old revelation is contrasted with the full and final revelation "in His Son." There is a progress, an evolution, to be discerned in the Old Testament religion. God spake to the Old Hebrew saints and worthies as they were able to receive His revelation. Some special aspect of religious truth is relative to the age which gives it birth. There is a progress from stage to stage. First one aspect of truth comes into prominence, then another. The new revelation often supersedes the old, when the old has played its part, and man is ready to receive fuller light. Our Lord Himself teaches us that there is this progress in revelation when He claims to supersede the teaching of the Old Testament: "Ye have heard that it was said to them of old time . . . . but

I say unto you . . ." (St. Matt. v. 21 ff.).   We must
not be surprised, therefore, if we find in the Old
Testament religious ideas and moral conceptions which
appear rudimentary and inadequate when placed side
by side with the teaching of our Lord and His Apostles
as recorded in the New Testament.   The former are
the scattered rays of the twilight of revelation; the
latter are the bright beams from the Sun of Righteousness which arose upon the world at the Incarnation
of Jesus Christ: and "when that which is perfect is
come, that which is in part shall be done away."

Again—and this particularly concerns us this
morning—God spake unto the fathers "in many
manners."   All kinds of methods by which the thought
of man takes shape in literary form are pressed into
the service of revelation in the Old Testament.   We
find there not merely history, and prophecy, and lyric
poetry; but we find also legend, and myth, and
dramatic poetry, and allegory.   And why should we
be surprised at this ?   Each of these types of literature
is a method by which it is given to the mind of one
man to make appeal to the minds of others; and
therefore it is meet that by every means revelation
should take shape and grow as it advances ever upward towards the perfect light.

And lastly, we observe that the author of Hebrews
connects the partial and fragmentary revelation of
the Old Testament with that to which it was all
along leading up: "God . . . hath at the end of
these days spoken unto us in His Son."   The Old

Testament must of necessity be read in the light of the New Testament in order that it may be understood. That must never for a moment be forgotten. Not, as we have already noticed, that we are to look for the religious ideals and moral standards of the New Testament, and expect to find them existing in their fully developed form in the Old Testament. But, that we shall find in the Old Testament a record of religious development, of religious revelation, which is absolutely unique of its kind ; and which can only rightly be read and understood when viewed as leading upward and pointing forward to the great revelation made in the fulness of time.

Having said so much about the character of the Old Testament revelation, and the literature in which it finds expression, let us pass on to deal more particularly with the early chapters of Genesis.

Now in the Book of Genesis we have to do with a work which is perhaps more puzzling and difficult to deal with than any other part of the Old Testament —at least until we have realized the true character of Old Testament revelation. Genesis, as dealing with the creation of the world, and the origins of the human race and of the Hebrew people in particular, is farthest removed from the normal sources of information which would be ready to an author's hand —sources such as historical records or written documents of any kind. We know now that, putting the book at the earliest possible date at which it could have been edited, or at which any of the documents of which the author made use could have been put into writing, the creation of the world must have taken place thousands, or, far more probably, millions of years earlier still. Even the diffusion of man upon the earth and the origin of the earliest civilizations of the East must have come about some thousands of years before any document contained in Genesis could have been written down. And coming down to later times, the movements of the more immediate ancestors of the Hebrew race, the patriarchs with whose history the book so largely deals, cannot be dated later than some hundreds of years before the earliest possible composition of any written document contained in Genesis.

It was no part of Inspiration to supply information which lies outside the sphere of *religious* truth, *i.e.* scientific and historical information as to the creation of the world and the origin of man upon it. Inspiration consists in God's putting into men's hearts thoughts and ideas as to the relationship of God to man, and the purpose which God has in view in placing man in the world and directing his actions. As the Second Epistle of St. Peter says, " No prophecy," —and by " prophecy " doubtless the writer means the religious teaching of all Scripture,—" no prophecy ever came by the will of man ; but men spake from God, being moved by the Holy Ghost " (2 Pet. i. 21). But when Inspiration, that is to say, divinely-directed religious teaching as to God's purpose with regard

to man, takes the form of a religious philosophy of
history, then the outward framework, the historical
form of the narrative, must be supplied through
human agency, by the best means which the writer
has at his resource.

What sources would such a writer be likely to have
at his disposal in giving a sketch of the creation of
the world and the earliest doings of humanity?

Doubtless in the earliest times, when men looked
out upon the world in which they were placed, they
reflected that it, like themselves, must have had
a beginning; and so, aided by the evidence which
Nature bears upon her face, they formed conjectures
as to the origin of all things—conjectures sometimes
wild and fantastic, sometimes more sober and reasoned,
and more nearly in accord with what science teaches
us at the present day. These conjectures were, as is
usual with primitive peoples, thrown into the form of
myths or allegories; and we know that such myths
as to creation were the common property of the
Semitic race, of which the Hebrews formed a part.
Such myths or allegorical presentations were, we shall
find, the medium through which the writer of Genesis
put forward his religious teaching as to the creation
of the world, the origin of mankind, and the existence
of sin which marred the relationship between God
and man. He found them, as we have noticed,
ready to his hand as the common property of the
Babylonians and other members of the stock from
which the Hebrews sprung; but he was divinely

guided to purge them of all elements which were
alien to the purpose which he had in hand—the
purpose of inculcating *religious truth* as suggested to
his mind by God's Holy Spirit.

So much may be affirmed in a general way about
the character of the sources employed in the early
chapters of Genesis.   Let us now consider more
particularly the religious lessons which are bound up
with them by the writer.   We are concerned this
morning with the story of the Fall; but the story of
Creation is connected with that so intimately that I
am bound first of all to say a few words with regard
to this latter.

We find the Hebrew story of Creation detailed
in Genesis, chs. i. and ii.   The order of events as
narrated in ch. i. cannot be squared with what
science has to tell us as to the process of creation,
even if we force the writer's language, and read into
it meanings which it cannot have been intended to
bear.   Various attempts have been made to form
such a harmony; but they must be admitted to be
failures, one and all.[1]   Even if we say that the six
days of creation figuratively describe six lengthy
periods of time, we still have to meet the difficulty
of accounting for the order of creative acts; and,
if we could gain a satisfactory solution of the order
of creation in ch. i., we are then confronted by the

[1] See the careful discussion in Driver, *Genesis* (*Westminster Commentary*), p. 19 ff.

fact that ch. ii., which comes from another source, gives an order which is in many respects different from that of ch. i., and which the final editor of Genesis has made no attempt to harmonize. There is a further fact to be considered, to which I have already alluded, namely, that we now possess an old Babylonian epic of creation, of a highly mythological character, which is closely connected in many points with the Hebrew narrative, and appears to have been the ultimate source of this latter.[1]

Yet, as we have already observed, these discrepancies between the Biblical narrative and the discoveries of science need not trouble us in the slightest degree. The writer was inspired to conceive and to convey *religious* truth, not miraculously to understand and to record scientific facts. He took, therefore, as the framework of the lessons which he had to convey, the old creation-myth which had grown up and been handed down from early ages, purged it of all that was offensive to his religious sense, and made it the medium of the truths which God's Holy Spirit put into his heart. Let us see very shortly what these truths are.

1. In the first place, the writer grasps the great fact of the unity of God, and His supremacy in creation. The fact is emphasized that all creation is dependent upon the one God. Before His *fiat* the

[1] The most complete edition of the Babylonian epic is that by L. W. King, *The Seven Tablets of Creation* (1902). On the points of connexion between this epic and the Hebrew narrative, see the commentaries of Driver, Skinner, and Ryle.

universe was non-existent: heaven and earth were called into being "in the beginning" of creation, *i.e.* at the beginning of time, which is the limit by which the range of human intellect is bounded. Before this beginning the writer simply assumes that God *is*, and therefore that He is by nature incomprehensible, eternal.

2. In the second place, Genesis repeatedly states that all things, as created by God, were *good*. We meet with the statement, many times repeated, "and God saw that it was good"; "and God saw everything that He had made, and, behold, it was very good." That is to say, all things, as created, are intended and thoroughly adapted to subserve the Divine Will. There is no trace of an eternal principle of evil. Nothing mars God's plan; nothing is the outcome of a struggle between two principles, the good and the bad.

In the grasping and statement of this fact we must surely find an extraordinary measure of inspiration on the part of this early writer. It is a fact which has often been doubted by those who fail to understand the great Fact of the Incarnation. There are so many things in the world as we know it which seem to tell against it. When we see, as the poet has it,

> "Nature red in tooth and claw
> With rapine";

when we see the human sorrow, pain, and failure which is around us, it is hard to realize that all things are intended to subserve the plan of a good God, were created to be "very good."

But, as you know, we have the answer to all such doubts in the Incarnation of the Son of God. What a failure, what a mockery of hopes would the life of Jesus Christ have been, if it had ended in the shame of the Cross! But in the Resurrection we have been permitted to see and to share in the outcome to which all along the pain and suffering were leading up; and we see this outcome to be "very good." And so, in answer to all doubts as to the goodness of God's providence in creation, our blessed Lord holds up the Crucifix, and assures us that "God so loved the world, that He gave His only-begotten Son"; and we are able, on the score of this great fact, to be sure that in the future all the anomalies of life will be cleared up and explained, when we shall see, no longer, as now, through a glass darkly, but face to face.

3. And, thirdly, the writer of Genesis is inspired to find in man the culmination of God's work. Man is formed in the divine image, fitted for communion with God. He has it in his power, apparently, to partake of the tree of life, and to live for ever; and it is only through a deliberate act of disobedience that he forfeits this high privilege. This brings us to the narrative of the Fall and its sequel, in which an allegorical setting serves to frame great spiritual truths, divinely taught.

We have, in the Babylonian myths, more than one story embodying speculation as to the reason why man failed to obtain the gift of immortality which was needed to make him like unto the gods. These stories, though they differ in details, have this in common, that they trace the failure to some accident or misfortune in no way under the control of man's conscious foresight. Genesis, on the contrary, finds the cause in a defect of the human will. Man, created in a state of innocent simplicity, sins through the rebellion of his free will; conscious freedom of choice being the endowment which he enjoys as formed in the image of God. The temptation comes from without. It is the serpent, the emblem of wisdom or cunning, which suggests the act of disobedience. The incentive is the desire for higher knowledge; to be "as God, knowing good and evil."

Here we have asserted the great truth which is emphasized in the New Testament that "sin is lawlessness" (1 St. John iii. 4). Sin is not, as some have thought it, undeveloped good, or a necessary accident in the process of human evolution. The Biblical doctrine of sin and the Fall does not, as stated in Genesis, contradict or conflict with the scientific theory of evolution. Genesis does not picture the first human pair as highly developed intellectual beings. It only postulates that at a certain stage the capacity of rational choice was introduced—the ability consciously to choose the good and to reject the evil; and that man, when he might have made the right choice, chose wrongly, and thereby entailed upon his descendants the heritage of the evil bent, the tendency to choose the evil.

Immediately upon the Fall there follow the passing and execution of the divine sentence. Adam and Eve, already conscious that they are unfit for the society of God, are driven forth from Eden. Pain and toil become thenceforth associated with the perpetuation and maintenance of human life; death, a return to the dust out of which man was taken, is decreed as its ending.

The religious value of the story is not vitiated by the fact that physical pain and death must have already existed in the world for ages past. Death, as the writer here regards it, is the culmination of man's spiritual separation from his Maker, the negation of that condition of spiritual communion with God to which man might have risen, could he have realized the possibility of perfect obedience to the will of God.

But the sentence is accompanied by a promise for the future of mankind. The curse pronounced upon the serpent ends with the statement, "I will put enmity between thee and the woman, and between thy seed and her seed: it shall bruise thy head, and thou shalt bruise his heel." This passage has rightly been named the *Protevangelium*. It contains more than an explanation of the natural hostility always existing between man and the serpent-race. It is a promise that, in the struggle of humanity with the spiritual power of evil, the seed of the woman shall

ultimately triumph. The bruising of the heel implies
that man shall not come unscarred out of the contest;
but the bruising of the head means the destruction of
the serpent—the final eradication of evil out of God's
creation. Here the writer grasps a great truth which
points forward to the Incarnation, and finds its fulfilment and satisfaction in it.

It is a commonplace of physical evolution that the
history of the race finds its short recapitulation in the
history of the individual. That is to say, the growth
of the individual from the embryo to the perfect form
summarizes the stages through which, in the course
of ages, man has attained his present development.
This is also true in the spiritual world, and not least
as regards the narrative of the Fall. To each of us
as individuals is given the power of conscious
voluntary choice, the possibility of choosing the good
and rejecting the evil. Each failure to respond to
the higher voice within us entails an evil bent in our
spiritual nature; the habit of sin becomes easier and
more natural to us, the choice of good more difficult.
For each of us the possibility of rising again to a new
life lies in the intervention of a higher Power, the gift
of the life of God within us which may grapple with
the power of evil and eradicate it from our nature.

That this is so has been, and still is, the spiritual
experience of many thousands: and in this fact we
surely may find the ultimate proof of the spiritual
insight of the old writer of Genesis; that is to say, of
his inspiration by God's Holy Spirit.

II.

THE TRIAL OF ABRAHAM.

"And Abraham called the name of that place *Jehovah yir'é*: as it is said to this day, In the mount of Jehovah provision shall be made."—GEN. xxii. 14.

OUR Lectionary prescribes the story of the great trial of Abraham's faith as the First Lesson for the morning of Good Friday. It is appropriate, therefore, that on this Sunday which opens our Holy Week we should take the narrative and think about it for a few minutes, endeavouring, so far as we can, to draw out its significance in the scheme of God's revelation to His chosen people, and to assess its character as a type and foreshadowing of that great Sacrifice which we are so soon to commemorate.

The story stands out from the pages of the Old Testament in more than one respect. As a piece of literature it is almost unique, even among so much in the narrative-portion of the Old Testament that must excite the admiration of all lovers of the masterpieces of descriptive writing. How telling is the severe restraint and simplicity which the narrator imposes upon himself in sketching, in a few brief sentences,

the divine command and the preparations unquestion-
ingly made by the patriarch for its fulfilment! The
words, " Thy son, thine only one, whom thou lovest,"
are pregnant with suggestion. In an instant there
lie revealed before us the tremendous scale of the
ordeal, the magnitude of the sacrifice demanded. As
in a flash, there pass through our mind the long years
of waiting for the precious gift, the hope at last
fulfilled beyond all expectation, the ideals which
centred themselves upon the life of that late-born
son, that he was to become the father of a mighty
nation, and that all the races of the world should be
blessed through him—then, in a moment, all to be
dashed to the ground, and that in the most awful
way by a deliberate act of surrender and renunciation.
And, in the simple narrative of Abraham's immediate
steps in response to God's behest, how much there is
which lies below the surface, unexpressed indeed in
words, yet, for the sympathetic reader, expressed to
the full by implication. The father acts ; he does
not speak. There is no question, no word of protest.
Just as some great river presents to outward view a
smooth unruffled surface, yet beneath that surface we
know that there rage mighty overwhelming currents ;
so we are left to imagine all the mental agony, the
straining of the father's heart-strings to the breaking
point, the blank despair of bereavement already
present in anticipation. It is as when some great
artist in black and white achieves his purpose with a
few bold strokes, putting a wealth of meaning into a

single line, where a smaller man would feel the necessity of elaborating his picture, achieving his results—such as they are—by a multitude of strokes and by great detail of light and shade ; yet, when the laboured composition is completed, it cannot for an instant compare with the severely simple masterpiece. So, we feel that our story is incomparable in the grandeur of its simplicity, and bears, in its austere restraint of words, the hall-mark of the true artist.

What a fine pathos, too, there is in the artless question of Isaac, and in Abraham's response : " My father, behold the fire and the wood : but where is the lamb for a burnt-offering ? " " God will provide Himself a lamb for a burnt-offering, my son." " The patriarch is beautifully depicted as maintaining his composure, unmoved by the question so innocently put to him by the unsuspecting boy, his only and dearly loved son. His obedience to God triumphs over the natural feeling of the father." [1] " God will provide Himself a lamb for a burnt-offering, my son." This ambiguous answer, intended primarily to keep the boy as long as possible unconscious of his impending fate, yet leaves room for the hope that God may at the last moment intervene, and prevent the awful tragedy.

The story is also prominent as marking a stage in the development of the religious thought of the Old Testament. It is—or should be—needless to say that the morality of God's command to Abraham is not to be judged by the standard of the present day—

[1] Knobel.

2

the standard of the New Testament. In the light of the full revelation of God's character vouchsafed to us by Jesus Christ, such a call for the sacrifice of an only son is clearly impossible—impossible, that is to say, in the form in which it came to Abraham, though the events of the present great crisis show us how it may come no less clearly in a somewhat different form. In reading the narrative we have to keep before our minds the fact that we are reading the record of a *development* in religious thought. God, as the author of the Epistle to the Hebrews reminds us, spake unto the fathers in the prophets—*i.e.* in the record of revelation contained in the Old Testament—"by many parts and in many manners," by a series of partial and, as it were, fragmentary revelations adapted to the times which gave them birth, revelations of some special aspect of truth vouchsafed to men's minds as they were able to receive them, but each in itself not the whole truth, as it has been granted to us in the full and final revelation made to us "in His Son," our Lord Jesus Christ.

Thus we are to judge the demand made upon Abraham's faith—upon his devotion to God—in the light of the times in which the patriarch lived. The custom of human sacrifice was, as we know, common among the nations of antiquity, and not least among the kindred races among whom Abraham's lot was cast. We, with our developed realization of the sanctity of human life, and the sanctity of the ties of human affection—the best of God's gifts, are naturally inclined to regard the practice solely from its hideously revolting aspect. But we should not blind our eyes to the fact that, in the underlying conception involved, there is the expression of a great truth, namely, that all that man possesses he owes to God, that no human possession should be counted too valuable, too precious, to be rendered up to the Creator and Sustainer of his being, and that, if the call should come for the greatest of all offerings, the greatest of all sacrifices, it must be made, readily and cheerfully.

So we picture Abraham seeing and hearing what went on around him among the peoples of Canaan in whose midst his lot was cast, conscious of the fact that on occasions these people were ready to offer to *their* deities this terrible and costly form of sacrifice ; and the thought must have crossed his mind whether *he* was ready to do as much for *his* God, the God who had shed His love upon him, who had taken him by the hand and led him from a far country, who had made him the object of a special providence, and poured out blessings and benefits upon him. Eventually, we may suppose, the questioning, perhaps at first vaguely recurrent, hardens itself into a *call*—a call all the more insistent for the cost which it entails, his only son in whom all his hopes and affections are wrapped up.

> " If Thou shouldst call me to resign
> What most I prize, it ne'er was mine ;
> I only yield Thee what is Thine ;
> Thy will be done."

In our narrative we have the outcome of the great mental struggle, and we learn that, though it was God's will that the testing should be made, and made to the full, it was not His will that it should take effect at this terrible cost. The father's hand is arrested at the last moment, and a substitute is provided. God is satisfied that the devotion of His servant is whole-hearted. "Now I know that thou fearest God, forasmuch as thou hast not withheld thy son, thine only one, from Me."

The writer of the Epistle to the Hebrews, in that incomparable chapter in which he reviews the acts of faith of the Old Testament saints, regards the sacrifice as completed, as in effect it *was*. "By faith Abraham, when he was tried, offered up Isaac: and he that had received the promises, offered up his only-begotten son, of whom it was said that, In Isaac shall thy seed be called: accounting that God was able to raise him up, even from the dead; from whence also he received him in a figure" (Heb. xi. 17–20).

The story of the testing of Abraham marks, as we have already noticed, a stage in the development of Old Testament thought, and that not, in itself, the highest stage which was reached. In its immediate application, it supplies the sanction for the custom which characterized the ritual requirements of Israel's religion, the abrogation of the sacrifice of a first-born son, and his redemption by the offering of an animal instead. In the case of Israel's great forefather, God had been pleased to provide for Himself an animal-

substitute for the more costly and terrible form of
sacrifice, and so it was taken to be His will that
human sacrifice should be abolished, and that the
offering of an animal should take its place. This is
a stage in advance; but not so high a stage as was
reached later on in the teaching of the prophets, who
grasped the great truth that it is not the actual
sacrifice at all which God requires, but the attitude of
mind and will towards God which it was intended to
typify. Witness the teaching of the prophet Micah,
who puts the anxious question into the mouth of the
Israelite of his time, and supplies the answer:

"Wherewith shall I come before Jehovah,
Or bow myself to God Most High?
Shall I come before Him with burnt-offerings,
With calves of a year old?
Will Jehovah be pleased with thousands of rams,
With myriads of rivers of oil?
Shall I give my first-born for my transgression,
The fruit of my body for the sin of my soul?
He hath shewed thee, O man, what is good;
And what doth Jehovah require of thee,
But to do justice and to love mercy,
And to walk humbly with thy God?"[1]

There is, however, more than this to be gathered
from the story of Abraham. It was not without good
cause that the lesson was chosen for Good Friday.
Without a doubt Abraham and his action are *typical*,
a faint foreshadowing of far greater events which were
to follow in the fulness of time. Probably the first
thought which animated the minds of those who made

[1] Mic. vi. 6-8.

choice of the lesson was the likeness of Abraham's offering of Isaac to the action of God the Father in sending His only-begotten Son into the world to die for our sins. " He that spared not His own Son, but delivered Him up for us all, how shall He not with Him also freely give us all things ? " (Rom. viii. 32). Still more closely, however, may we parallel the attitude of mind displayed by Abraham with the attitude of our Lord Himself at the supreme crisis. The victory was won, but not, as we know, without a struggle of the human feelings to bring the will into entire subservience to the will of God. " O My Father, if it be possible, let this cup pass away from Me ; nevertheless, not as I will, but as Thou wilt " (St. Matt. xxvi. 39).

And so, in times of suffering, stress, and trial like the present time, the great example is handed down for us to follow ; and the strength, too, is offered which can enable us to win through to the end, like the Captain of our salvation. " In that He Himself hath suffered, being tested, He is able to succour them that are tested " (Heb. ii. 18).

" Abraham called the name of that place Jehovah *yir'é*." The Hebrew phrase means, " *Jehovah sees*," *i.e. foresees* or *makes provision*. In its immediate application, the name goes back to the patriarch's answer to his son, " God will provide Himself a lamb for a burnt-offering, my son "—an unconscious prophecy, destined to be fulfilled beyond all hope by the staying of Abraham's hand and the provision of a ram for a sacrifice. The narrator adds, however, that the name passed into a proverbial saying, which was current at his own day— " as it is said to this day, In the mount of Jehovah provision shall be made."

Here "the mount of Jehovah" means the Temple-mount, the supreme centre of God's Self-manifestation, the seat of His earthly dwelling. So used, *Jehovah yir'é* means, I take it, in its fullest application, that the issues of life and death, which to us seem dark, tangled, and confused, are, for God, *clear-cut*. God foresees, and makes provision. For those who trust in God, and who strive with full intent to place their wills into entire subservience to *His* will, nothing happens by chance. They cannot, they may not, feel that they are the sport of circumstance, the victims of fate. Is there a difficulty which harasses the mind, a grief which tears the heart ? Take it up to the mount of the Lord. Jehovah sees. Jehovah will provide. In the mount of the Lord provision shall be made.

In the great events which we are to commemorate this week it has pleased God to lift the veil, and to allow us to see the issue of His divine plan. Supposing that, so far as we knew, Good Friday had witnessed the end of Jesus Christ's life, and the outcome of it all had been withheld from our human understanding, what a failure, what a tragedy it must all have seemed ! But the veil, thank God, *has* been lifted, and we have been allowed to witness the glorious Resurrection. We see the issue of the great struggle, the victory. We know of a truth that Jesus Christ is the very Paschal Lamb which was offered for us, and hath taken away the sin of the world; who by His death hath destroyed death, and by His rising to life again hath restored to us everlasting life.

Can we not trust that, in the trials and difficulties of our earthly life—not least, in the present great ordeal through which we are passing—the outcome, could we foresee it, will be not dissimilar? "In the mount of the Lord provision shall be made."

III.

THE NAME JEHOVAH AND ITS MEANING.

"And God said moreover unto Moses, Thus shalt thou say unto the children of Israel, Jehovah, the God of your fathers, the God of Abraham, the God of Isaac, and the God of Jacob, hath sent me unto you: this is My name for ever, and this is My memorial unto all generations."—Ex. iii. 15.

THE splendid chapter which we read as the First Lesson this morning records one of the greatest incidents—perhaps *the* greatest incident—in the history of Old Testament religion. In it we have the account of God's revelation of Himself to Moses under *a new name*, the name which is to be regarded as pre-eminently *the proper name* of Israel's God, and which is commonly represented in English under the form *Jehovah*. I want to speak for a little this morning about this name, and its importance as *the name of revelation*.

In order to make what I have to say as clear as I can, it is necessary that I should first of all allude briefly to the fact that the first five books of the Bible which we call the Pentateuch are not the work of a single author, but have been formed by the weld-

ing together of several originally distinct narratives.
Of these, the Book of Deuteronomy stands by itself as
a single whole. Throughout the other books *three*
narratives can be traced. The two oldest of these
are based on very early traditions, which were
probably for a long period handed down by word of
mouth. They seem to have taken shape in written
form at the hands of the prophetic schools or guilds
which we know to have existed in Israel during the
period of the monarchy. In their original form, they
were probably continuous histories of the past from
the earliest times down to the days of David (for they
seem to find their continuation in the Books of Joshua,
Judges, and 1 Samuel), and they appear to have
emanated, the one from the Southern Kingdom of
Judah, the other from the Northern Kingdom of
Israel. These two histories, which covered very much
the same ground, were subsequently welded into one
—a process which involved a certain amount of
omission from the one or the other where the matter
which they contained was common to both, though
considerable repetition was allowed to remain. Later
still, the combined narrative was worked up with a
third narrative written from a priestly and juristic
point of view, and mainly interested in the origin of
legal institutions, and in genealogies and other
statistical matter. The final welding of the narratives
into a single whole, and the inclusion with them
of the Book of Deuteronomy, which produced the
Pentateuch as it has come down to us, did not take

place until the days of Ezra, after the return from exile.

I mention these facts in order to explain how it is that, while our narrative of God's revelation made to Moses seems to picture the name Jehovah as a *new* name, marking a new phase of revelation, yet we find the name occurring with frequency in the Book of Genesis. The reason is that one of the old history-books—that which was composed in the kingdom of Judah—pictures the use of the name as primeval, employing it in the narrative of Creation in Gen. ii., and stating in Gen. iv. 26 that in the days of Enosh, the grandson of Adam, "men began to call on the name of Jehovah," or, as the passage should more correctly be rendered, "to call *by* the name of Jehovah," *i.e.* to use the name in invocation. The north Israelite history-book, on the other hand, from which comes the main strand of the narrative which we read as the First Lesson, consistently avoids the use of the name Jehovah throughout Genesis, up to its account of the revelation of the name to Moses in Ex. iii., always using, in the earlier history, the word which means "*God.*" This is also the case with the third narrative, which we may call the Priestly narrative; for it is from this narrative that the passage comes which we find in Ex. vi. 2, 3, where God says to Moses, "I am *Jehovah*: and I appeared unto Abraham, unto Isaac, and unto Jacob, as *God Almighty*, but by My name *Jehovah* I was not known unto them." This narrative, then, pictures stages of revelation marked by the promulgation of different divine names—first the name *Elōhîm* or *God*, which is used by the writer in the narrative of Creation which we find in Gen. i. ; then the name *El Shaddai*, rendered *God Almighty*, which occurs first in God's revelation to Abraham recorded in Gen. xvii., " I am God Almighty ; walk before Me, and be thou perfect "; finally, the name *Jehovah*, revealed in its fulness of meaning to Moses at Mount Sinai.

It does not follow, because one tradition pictures the name Jehovah as known and used from the earliest times, whereas the other regards it as a new revelation to Moses, that therefore one is historically correct, and the other incorrect. As a matter of fact, external information supplied by Babylonian documents has shown that the name was known and used in very early times, and among a wider circle of peoples than Israel, just as the old Judæan document pictures it as being known. But, on the other hand, it is quite certain that the name, as thus used, was not thought of as containing the fulness of meaning with which it was interpreted to Moses in the revelation at Mount Sinai. Previously unknown to and unused by the Israelites in Egypt, it was given to Moses invested with a new meaning—a meaning which, as we shall proceed to notice, marked it out pre-eminently as the name of revelation ; and from that day onwards it came to be regarded as *the* name *par excellence* of Israel's God.

Before speaking, however, of the *meaning* of the name Jehovah, it is worth while to notice very briefly the reason why it occurs so rarely in its Hebrew form in our English versions. Usually we find it translated as " the LORD "; and wherever in the English Bible you find LORD or GOD printed in capital letters *throughout*, it stands for this divine Name in the original. The rendering " LORD " does not, however, give us the true meaning of *Jehovah*.

The reason for its adoption is as follows. There are certain enactments in the Jewish law which are aimed against profane or frivolous usage of the holy Name. Chief among these is the third commandment, " Thou shalt not take the name of Jehovah thy God in vain," the sense of which would perhaps be better expressed if we were to render it, " Thou shalt not *utter* the name of Jehovah *lightly*." This was interpreted by the Jews of post-exilic times as forbidding the very mention of the divine Name, even in the public reading of the Scriptures; and so there grew up the custom of substituting the title *Adonay*, which means " the Lord," or rather " my Lord," wherever the divine Name occurred in the Old Testament; unless it stood in connexion with the word meaning " Lord " (as in the expression " Lord Jehovah," which is frequent in Ezekiel), in which case the word meaning " God " was substituted. This practice has been followed in the Greek and Latin versions of the Hebrew Old Testament, and has hence made its way, for the most part, into our English Bible, though, as we have already noticed, there are a few passages in which *Jehovah* is retained.

The Jewish avoidance of the pronunciation of the divine Name was so thoroughgoing that no Jewish tradition exists as to its original form. The conventional form Jehovah is really a mixed form, consisting of a combination of the four consonants of the name JHVH, or to give the letters their true sound YHWH, with the vowels of *Adonay*, the word meaning *Lord*. Hebrew, when it was a living, spoken language, was written in consonants merely, the correct vowels being understood through knowledge of the grammatical forms. After it ceased to be the ordinary spoken language of the Jews, the need was felt of indicating in writing its correct vocalic pronunciation, in order to facilitate the reading of the Lessons in the Synagogue; and at length a system of vowel-points was invented, and these were added in MSS above and below the consonants. The scholars who added the vowel-points wished to indicate that *Adonay* or "Lord" was to be substituted for the divine Name in public reading, but they did not venture to alter the four consonants of the name. Thus they simply added the vowels of *Adonay* to the four sacred consonants in order to indicate that the change was to be made, never contemplating that the consonants themselves would be pronounced in combination with the vowels of this other word. As a matter of fact, the Name was never pronounced as Jehovah until comparatively modern times, this form

being first introduced in the sixteenth century of our
era by a monk named Petrus Galatinus. The original
pronunciation of the Name may be gathered partly
from Samaritan tradition and partly from grammatical
considerations; and such evidence points to an original
form Jahveh or Yahweh. The conventional form
Jehovah has, however, gained for us a certain sanctity
through long usage; and we may retain that form in
speaking of the Name.

Now as to the meaning of the Name as revealed
to Moses. This is explained by the verse which,
as rendered in the English Bible, runs, "And God
said unto Moses, *I am that I am*: and He said, Thus
shalt thou say unto the children of Israel, *I am* hath
sent me unto you." We ought, however, to translate
the explanatory phrase, not "*I am that I am*," but,
"*I will become what I will become.*" Here we have
the first person of the verb "to become" used to
explain a form which is itself regarded as the third
person of the verb. "*He who becomes*," or "*He who
will become*," *i.e.* the God who is and will be constantly manifesting Himself to Israel through a
progressive series of revelations: and the statement,
"*I will become what I will become*," seems to indicate
that no words can adequately sum up all that Jehovah
will become to His chosen people, that they are to be
the recipients of a series of revelations each in itself,
it may be, partial and fragmentary, but belonging
none the less to the series of progress "by many parts
and in many manners," of which the writer of the

Epistle to the Hebrews speaks, and ever tending upwards towards the perfect manifestation of our Lord Jesus Christ.

Now, does not the conception involved in the meaning of this name at once tend to ease and to explain the difficulties which people sometimes find in the reading of the Old Testament, namely, the fact that the moral standards therein contained often seem to be defective and imperfect when compared with the Christian standard as set forth by our Lord? Readers of the Bible have often imagined that the morality of the Old Testament should be on a level with that of the New Testament, and they have been troubled by the moral difficulties which on this view are bound to stare them in the face. How could a righteous and holy God have been thought to command such acts as Abraham's sacrifice of Isaac, or the total extirpation of the Canaanite nations— to quote two points merely among many others which suggest themselves? The answer, of course, is that the Israelite religion of those early times was as yet at a comparatively low level, high indeed as compared with the religion of surrounding nations, yet still but the twilight of revelation, not to be compared, in fulness and finality, with the revelation vouchsafed to us by Jesus Christ. "God spake unto the fathers in the prophets (*i.e.* in the Old Testament as a whole) by many parts and in many manners." It was indeed the divine voice which spoke, but it spoke to men as they were able to understand it at a low stage of development, and they often misunderstood or understood but imperfectly.

It is the record of a gradual religious evolution to which the Old Testament witnesses, albeit that it is an evolution guided and providentially designed by God Himself. Thus we find in the Old Testament itself older ideas as to God's relationship towards man gradually superseded by newer and truer ideas owing to the progress of revelation. And, when we come to the teaching of our Lord, we find that in many respects He claims to set aside and to supersede the standards of the Old Testament. "Ye have heard that it was said to them of old time . . . but I say unto you . . ." (St. Matt. v. 21 ff.). Or again, when the disciples, St. James and St. John, quote the precedent of Elijah for calling down fire from heaven upon the Samaritan village which refused admittance to our Lord, we read that He turned and rebuked them (St. Luke ix. 51–56).

Why, then,—it may perhaps be asked at this stage, —do we read the Old Testament in church, if so much that it contains consists of the partial sidelights of revelation, and was rendered obsolete by the revelation of Jesus Christ? The answer is to be found in the fact that it was the Bible of our Lord, the object of His constant study, as is clear from the way in which He so repeatedly refers to it. While it is true that, on the one hand, He claims to supersede some of its moral standards, it is also true that He regards it as pointing forward to Himself. "One jot

3

or one tittle shall in no wise pass from the Law until
all be fulfilled " (St. Matt. v. 18). " Search the scriptures ; for in them ye think that ye have eternal life :
and they are they which testify of Me " (St. John v. 39).
Thus these Old Testament scriptures, to which our
Lord, of course, is referring, have a permanent value
for us as the record of a gradual revelation leading
up to Jesus Christ and pointing forward to Him.
Again, while we find in the Old Testament as a
whole the record of a gradual revelation, there can
be no doubt that much of the teaching which it
contains reaches a spiritual level which can never be
surpassed or superseded, and which can be taken over
into the Christian religion as the moral standard of
action and the expression of the highest spiritual
aspiration of the human soul in relation to God.
This is especially true of the teaching of the Prophets
and the Psalms.   We recollect how our Lord Himself
used the words of two of the Psalms as the expression
of the deepest feelings of His soul in relation to God
the Father at the supreme crisis of His earthly life
when He hung upon the Cross ; or, again, we remember
how He turned aside the temptations of the evil one
by three separate appeals to that deeply spiritual
book, the Book of Deuteronomy.

Again, it may be asked, how are we to know what
part of the teaching of the Old Testament is of permanent spiritual value, and what of a merely partial
and provisional character ?   Partly by bringing it to
the touchstone of the teaching of our Lord as recorded

in the New Testament, and partly by the verdict of
our conscience, *i.e.* the voice of the living Christ
within us as interpreted to us by the action of His
Holy Spirit. This latter aspect of the spiritual
appeal of the Old Testament has been well summed
up by S. T. Coleridge in his *Letters on the Inspiration
of the Scriptures.* "Need I say," he remarks, "that
I have met everywhere more or less copious sources
of truth, and power, and purifying impulses; that I
have found words for my inmost thoughts, songs for
my joy, utterances for my hidden griefs, and pleadings
for my shame and my feebleness? In short, whatever *finds* me, bears witness for itself that it has
proceeded from a Holy Spirit, 'which, remaining in
itself, yet regenerateth all other powers, and in all
ages entering into holy souls maketh them friends of
God and prophets'" (Wisd. vii. 27).

To sum up. We read the Old Testament in
church for two reasons. (1) As an historical record
of the process of divine revelation in old time, leading
up to the New Testament revelation. Thus, as
pointing forward to and finding its fulfilment in the
New Testament, it may be regarded as evidential
of the truth of Christianity. (2) As of practical
spiritual value for the present needs of our souls.
From this point of view the distinction between
what is imperfect and transitory and what is of
permanent truth and application must be judged
by the conscience of the individual reader as enlightened by the revelation of our Lord.

Both these points of view come under the head of *edification, i.e.* the building up of our souls in our most holy Faith. It is obvious, however, that, to secure such edification in its highest degree, the selection of the chapters to be publicly read should be a matter of great care, and that in this regard our present Lectionary is in many points susceptible of revision. Such a revision has been carefully and skilfully made in the new Lectionary which is now under consideration in the two Houses of Convocation, and it is much to be hoped that it may shortly be legalized and adopted. We do not want to read in church about the bloodthirsty revolution of Jehu. We want more of the practical moral and social teaching of the Prophets; more of the high spiritual teaching of Deuteronomy, which finds in the love of God the mainspring of human action, entering into all the relations of life; we want the fine old patriarchal traditions of Genesis, in which we have worked out the idea that a man can feel that he stands in such a moral relation to God that he is able to commit the whole guidance of his life to Him, to feel that he is an instrument in God's hands for the performance of His will, that each and all of his actions are not too trivial to come within the range of this all-embracing relation, and, so doing, to be directed, inspired, heightened, and purified. And (may we not add?) we need some of those incomparable narratives of the later historical books, which, for sheer beauty of style and vividness of expression, uplift our souls like the finest poetry or the finest music. Take only one example—the words of Ruth to Naomi:

> "Intreat me not to leave thee,
> And to return from following after thee :
> For where thou goest, I will go ;
> And where thou lodgest, I will lodge :
> Thy people shall be my people,
> And thy God my God :
> Where thou diest, will I die,
> And there will I be buried :
> The Lord do so to me, and more also,
> If ought but death part thee and me."

We could not spare such a passage as that, for it is surely unrivalled in all literature.

One last thought before I close. The name Jehovah expresses, as we have seen, the great fact of God's gradual Self-revelation. All through Israel's history He was "He who will become," the God who was progressively manifesting His nature and His divine purpose in the shaping of the nation's destiny.

Has He, however, after the full and final revelation of His character made to the world in the Person of Jesus Christ, ceased to be for us *the God who will become* ? I think not. Granted that in Jesus Christ we have all that mankind needs to know about the character of God, yet there are new applications of that character, of that teaching, suited to every age and every condition of society. This at any rate is the view of the two great theologians of the New

Testament, St. John and St. Paul. It is St. John who has preserved for us the words of our Lord in regard to the action of the Holy Spirit as the interpreter to men's minds of the inexhaustible meaning of His teaching. "When He, the Spirit of truth, is come, He shall guide you into all truth: for He shall not speak from Himself; but whatsoever things He shall hear, these shall He speak: and He shall declare unto you the things that are to come. He shall glorify Me: for He shall take of Mine, and shall declare it unto you" (St. John xvi. 13, 14). These words are intended to apply, not merely to the Apostles, but to all true members of Christ's Church, all down the ages. To St. Paul, again, the power of the living Christ, guiding, directing, exhorting, was such a reality that in face of it he seems almost to relegate appeal to the historical Christ to a secondary position—"even though we have known Christ after the flesh, yet now henceforth know we Him no more. Wherefore, if any man is in Christ, he is a new creature. The old things are passed away; behold, they are become new" (2 Cor. v. 16, 17).

That is the real strength of Christianity, the appeal to the living Christ, still working in men's hearts, still manifesting Himself with an appeal which is ever new, ever suited to every occasion, every crisis which may arise in the history of the world. We as a Church need to realize this more and more, ever listening for the divine Spirit, ever ready to adjust and to expand our point of view to meet fresh needs, and, like wise householders, bringing forth out of our treasury things both new and old.

Thus the great name Jehovah, " He who will become," has still its ever-present application for this and future ages: " This is My name for ever, and this is My memorial unto all generations "—and that is the hope of the world.

IV.

THE CROSSING OF THE RED SEA.

"And the Lord said unto Moses, Wherefore criest thou unto Me? Speak unto the children of Israel that they go forward." —Ex. xiv. 15.

THE narrative of Israel's deliverance from Egypt is taken in the New Testament as typical of the great events of Good Friday and Easter Day; and it is for this reason that the Old Testament lessons for Easter Day are selected from this narrative —in the morning the account of the institution of the Passover, the blood-shedding of the lamb without blemish and without spot procuring atonement for Israel, a type of the great fact that "Christ our Passover is sacrificed for us"; in the evening, the account of the crossing of the Red Sea, the breaking once and for all of the yoke of Egypt, and the birth of Israel as a nation and as a Church, typical of our Saviour's triumph over the power of evil, His breaking once and for all the yoke of sin and the Devil, and the birthday of the Christian Church. The typology of this latter event is worked out in the New Testament, especially by St. Paul, in a number

THE CROSSING OF THE RED SEA

of passages. It will be sufficient now to allude to the fact that this Apostle finds, in the crossing of the Red Sea, a type of baptism as the act of incorporation into the Christian Church, Moses the initiator of the Old Dispensation being the counterpart of Christ the initiator of the New Dispensation—" all our fathers were under the cloud, and all passed through the sea, and all were baptized into Moses in the cloud and in the sea" (1 Cor. x. 2). So, too, in the vision of the writer of the Book of Revelation, it is said of those who have been redeemed from the bondage of sin that, like the Israelites redeemed from the bondage of Egypt, " They sing the song of Moses the servant of God, and the song of the Lamb, saying, Great and marvellous are Thy works, O Lord God Almighty ; just and true are Thy ways, Thou King of the ages. Who shall not fear Thee, O Lord, and glorify Thy name ? For Thou only art holy : for all nations shall come and bow themselves before Thee ; for Thy judgments are made manifest " (Rev. xv. 3, 4).

The story of the passage of the Red Sea has received remarkable confirmation in modern times through observation of the phenomena of nature. The action of a strong gale of wind upon shallow water has not infrequently been known to produce results not unlike those which are recorded in the Biblical narrative. For instance, it is stated that, in the year 1738, the Russians entered the Crimea, which was strongly held against them by the Turks, by means of a passage made by the wind through the shallow waters of the Putrid sea, at the north-west corner of the Sea of Azov. And similarly, in Egypt itself, a strong east wind—the wind which is mentioned in our narrative—has been known to cause the waters of the great lake at the northern end of the Suez Canal to recede for a distance of seven miles, leaving a stretch of bare sand.[1]

God works ordinarily, by adapting natural laws to serve His divine purpose. The plagues of Egypt can be explained as aggravated instances of natural scourges to which Egypt is peculiarly liable. This is a consideration which, while it tends to confirm the historical truth of the Biblical narrative, in no way diminishes the value of the phenomena as signal instances of the divine interposition. Proof of the divine working is to be seen in the occurrence of these events at a particular crisis in Israel's history, for the effecting of a particular purpose. And the fact that Israel was right in seeing in them the direct intervention of the hand of God may be read in the part which the nation was destined, in the divine providence, to play in the history of the world.

In ancient times, so geologists tell us, the waters of the Red Sea extended much farther to the north than they do at present, the former extension of the Gulf of Suez being now marked by a series of lakes

[1] See Rendel Harris and Chapman, in Hastings' *Dictionary of the Bible*, i. p. 802[b].

along the line of the Suez Canal. As one travels
by railway to Cairo and approaches the station of
Isma'iliya, one catches a glimpse of the blue waters
of Lake Timsâh gleaming across the yellow sand-dunes
and the brown tufts of desert-vegetation. It was
probably somewhere in this neighbourhood that the
children of Israel, encamped over against the sea,
became aware that Pharaoh had changed his mind,
that he had summoned an army and was in hot
pursuit of them, resolved to intercept them and to
compel their return to bondage. All hope of
escape seemed to be cut off—" the foe behind, the
deep before." They were, as yet, a race of slaves,
and they could not in a moment rise to the dignity
of their vocation and to trust in their divinely
appointed leader. We read that " they were sore
afraid." Bitterly, in their despair, they turned upon
Moses and reproached him. " Because there were
no graves in Egypt, hast thou taken us away to die
in the wilderness ? Wherefore hast thou thus dealt
with us, to bring us forth out of Egypt ? Is not this
the word that we spake unto thee in Egypt, saying,
Let us alone that we may serve the Egyptians ? For
it were better for us to serve the Egyptians, than
that we should die in the wilderness." Moses,
however, answered with calm confidence, " Fear ye
not, stand still and see the salvation of the Lord,
which He will work for you to-day ; for the Egyptians
whom ye have seen to-day, ye shall see them again
no more for ever. The Lord shall fight for you, and

ye shall hold your peace." And then follows the
divine command which we have taken as our text,
"Speak unto the children of Israel that they go
forward."

You are familiar with the sequel. You know how
night fell, hiding the two hosts one from the other,
and how all night long a strong east wind blew,
sweeping back the waters of the gulf, so that, at dawn
of day, Israel found a way prepared for their crossing
over in safety. Then, as the Egyptian host essayed the
same feat, the wind suddenly fell or veered, so that the
waters returned once more to their normal channel,
and the foe was overwhelmed. "Thus the Lord saved
Israel that day out of the hand of the Egyptians;
and Israel saw the Egyptians dead upon the seashore.
And Israel saw the great work which the Lord did
upon the Egyptians, and the people feared the Lord:
and they believed in the Lord, and in His servant
Moses" (Ex. xiv. 31).

It was not, we may believe, a mere coincidence that
twelve hundred years later, at precisely the same season,
the Passion of our Lord fell upon the Passover Eve—
that He, the true Passover Lamb, suffered and died for
our salvation at the very moment when the Jews
were making ready for their annual commemoration of
the Passover feast; and, again, that He rose victorious
from the tomb on the third day, breaking once and
for all the power of sin and death, upon the anniversary
of the crossing of the Red Sea, the breaking of the

yoke of Egyptian bondage, and the birth of Israel as a nation.

Now again, after some nineteen hundred years, at precisely the same season, we find ourselves in the throes of a world-crisis; and was it merely a coincidence that the week of our Saviour's Passion was for us the very acme of suffering, anxiety, and dread as to the issue of events,[1] and that, as Easter dawned, there seemed to dawn for us the glimmer of a brighter day, the beginning of a hope, God-given, that the foe is destined to shatter himself in vain against our lines, and that, in reliance upon the justice of our cause, its sanctification as the cause of righteousness and freedom, we shall eventually destroy his power? To me, at any rate, as I read that chapter in Exodus at last Sunday's Evensong, it came home with a new meaning, a new note of inspiration—" Fear ye not, stand still, and see the salvation of the Lord, which He will work for you to-day. . . . The Lord shall fight for you, and ye shall hold your peace."

To us, no doubt, there comes home at this time the command to co-operate with the divine plan— " Speak unto the children of Israel that they go forward." There were, as we have seen, pessimists and defeatists many enough within the ranks of Israel, those in whose nature the spirit of slaves was deeply ingrained, to whom it seemed easier and safer to bow

[1] The great German advance, March 21, 1918, was the Thursday of Passion Week. The extreme tension continued throughout Holy Week.

their backs to the taskmaster's lash than to stake all
upon a great adventure.   But the heart of the nation
must have been sound; at any rate, by God's grace,
they were caught and fired by the spirit of their
great leader and, men, women, and children, *they
went forward.*

Let us take the lesson, and apply it to ourselves;
now especially when the call comes so insistently to
all ranks and classes among us, "Speak unto the
children of Israel that they go forward." By and
by—it may not be at once, but can we doubt
that it will be so in the long run, and the sooner,
doubtless, in proportion to the faith and alacrity
with which we obey the summons?—it may be
given to us to sing the song of Moses the servant
of God:

"I will sing unto the Lord, for He hath triumphed
    gloriously,
The horse and his rider hath He whelmed in the sea.
The Lord is my strength and song,
And He is become my salvation.

.   .   .   .

Thy right hand, O Lord, is glorious in power;
Thy right hand, O Lord, shattereth the foe.
And in the greatness of Thine excellency Thou over-
    throwest Thine adversaries:
Thou sendest forth Thy wrath, it consumeth them like
    chaff.

.   .   .   .

The enemy said, I will pursue, I will overtake,
I will divide the spoil, my lust shall be satisfied upon
    them;
I will draw my sword, my hand shall destroy them.

Thou didst blow with Thy wind, the sea covered them,
They sank like lead in the mighty waters.
Who is like unto Thee, O Lord, among the gods?
Who is like Thee, glorious in holiness,
Fearful in praises, doing wonders?

.   .   .   .

The Lord shall reign for ever and ever."

V.

AHAB AND BEN-HADAD.

"And he said unto him, Thus saith the Lord, Because thou hast let go out of thy hand the man whom I had devoted to destruction, therefore thy life shall go for his life, and thy people for his people.—1 KINGS xx. 42.

THE First Lessons appointed for last Sunday and this Sunday deal with the period of Israel's struggle with the neighbouring kingdom of Syria. The Biblical narrative is, from an historical point of view, intensely interesting, more especially because we are able considerably to supplement it by information derived from the annals of the contemporary Assyrian king, Shalmaneser III., which actually mention Ben-Hadad, king of Syria, and Ahab, king of Israel, and throw fresh light upon their relations one with the other.

I have chosen to speak about the narrative this morning, because the lessons which it has to teach seem to me peculiarly apposite to the stage which we have reached in the present world-conflict. It would be possible, had we the time and opportunity, to treat it in its bearing upon the political and military situation in the nearer East. Lines of communication and other geographical factors form a permanent element in the situation in Western Asia, and the political movements of the 9th century B.C. (the period of Ahab) have their value as illustrating and forecasting the political movements of the present day in the same district. This, however, is a subject which lies outside the scope of a sermon; and which would, moreover, absorb far too much time, and require the use of a map for its full elucidation. I shall only allude to this aspect of the subject in so far as it is necessary for the right understanding of our narrative.

The picturesque narratives which occupy the middle part of the Book of Kings, extending from 1 Kings xvii. to 2 Kings x., and including 2 Kings xiii. 14–21, are all the work of members of the prophetic schools or guilds of the Northern kingdom of Israel. They fall, roughly speaking, into two classes—narratives which may be classed as lives of the prophets Elijah and Elisha, and narratives which have to do, in the main, with the political history of Israel in relation to Syria. Both classes of narrative are ancient, and must have been written down not long after the events which they narrate; but those which deal with the history of the kingdom are relatively the older, and bear more nearly the character of literal history. 1 Kings xx., from which our text is taken, has as its immediate sequel 1 Kings xxii., which we read as the First Lesson last Sunday—the story of the death of Ahab in the battle

4

of Ramoth-Gilead. Chapter xxi., which gives us the
story of Naboth's vineyard, has been wrongly inter-
polated between the two chapters, and should properly
follow ch. xix., which, with chs. xvii. and xviii.,
belongs to the narrative of the life of Elijah. The
error in arrangement has come about in the Hebrew
text from which our English version is translated;
but the correct order of chapters is still preserved in
the Greek version, which goes back to an older
Hebrew original.

In speaking of Israel's relations with the Syrians
— or, to give them their more correct title, the
Aramæans—it is necessary to make brief reference
to the geographical position occupied by the two
peoples.

The eastern coast-land of the Mediterranean—the
country which we call Palestine and Syria—is a fertile
strip backed to the east by the desert. It is only in
the extreme north that this strip joins hands, as it
were, with another fertile and settled country, the
land of Mesopotamia, which is watered by the two
great rivers, the Euphrates to the west and the Tigris
to the east; and the Syrian desert forms, roughly
speaking, a triangle interposed between the two
countries. It was at the apex of this triangle that
there clustered, at the times of which we are
speaking, a number of small Syrian or Aramæan
States, extending from the upper waters of the
Euphrates south-westward through northern Syria
to the Lebanon district, to the east of which was

Assyrian armies sweep by along the maritime plain of the Mediterranean towards Egypt, which was their ultimate objective. The prophets of Israel cared nothing for worldly aggrandizement—rather, we may say, they were opposed to it. They favoured plain living and high thinking in the best sense. Their aim for their country was that she should cultivate her internal resources, which were largely agricultural, and keep her religion and moral life pure and unspotted from the world.

The beginning of our narrative in 1 Kings xx. presupposes the prior narration of events at which, in the absence of direct information, we can only guess. Ahab, and his father Omri before him, had probably undergone a galling vassalage to Ben-Hadad; and possibly an attempt made by Ahab to escape from this vassalage had led to defeat in the field, and driven him to take refuge in Samaria. In any case, the narrative opens with the investiture of Samaria by the Syrian army, and the sending by Ben-Hadad of humiliating terms of surrender: "Thus saith Ben-Hadad, thy silver and thy gold is mine; thy wives also and thy children, even the goodliest, are mine." Ahab is obviously at the end of his resources, and can do nothing but acquiesce. He replies with Oriental servility, "It is according to thy saying, my lord the king; I am thine and all that I have." This, however, does not suffice Ben-Hadad. He is determined to inflict the greatest possible amount of humiliation upon his conquered foe; so he expresses his intention of sending his servants on the morrow to search the palace of Ahab and the houses of his subjects, and to carry off everything to which they may attach a value.

This was an indignity to which Ahab could hardly submit. After consultation with his ministers, he sends back a courteously-worded refusal, and thereby provokes from Ben-Hadad a threat which recalls to our mind the Kaiser's reference to "French's contemptible little army"—"The gods do so unto me, and more also, if the dust of Samaria shall suffice for handfuls for all the people that follow me." To this Ahab replied simply, "Tell him, Let not him that girdeth on his armour boast himself as he that putteth it off"—a proverb the force of which has been realized not a few times in history, and is, as we believe and trust, about to be realized again in the present great conflict.

We need not enter in detail into what followed. Suffice it to say that a successfully-planned sortie, made when Ben-Hadad was carousing with his officers, in confidence that he could reduce the city at his leisure, led to the rout of the Syrian host, the king himself barely escaping capture.

Next year the Syrians again invaded the land of Israel, a pitched battle was fought, and Israel was victorious. Ben-Hadad could only gain a temporary place of concealment. After hurried consultation his servants propose a plan of action. "Behold, now," they say, "we have heard that the kings of the house

of Israel are merciful kings; prithee let us put
sackcloth on our loins, and ropes upon our heads, and
go out to the King of Israel: peradventure he will
spare thy life." The plan is adopted. In this captive
garb they meet Ahab, and intercede for their master's
life—"Thy servant Ben-Hadad saith, I pray thee let
me live." Ahab, in generous mood, replies, "Is he
yet alive? He is my brother"; and the envoys at
once divine his mood and catch at his words, repeating
the phrase, "Thy *brother*, Ben-Hadad." Forthwith,
Ben-Hadad is fetched from his concealment, and taken
up by Ahab into his chariot, and we have an example
of peace by negotiation. The Syrian king is profuse
in his promises. The Israelite cities which his father
took from Ahab's father Omri are to be returned, and
Ahab is to have the right of making streets or
bazaars in Damascus, just as the former Ben-Hadad
had made them in Samaria. We observe that Ben-
Hadad had still, as the phrase goes, all the cards in his
hands, since the cities, though promised, were still in
his possession, and he was suffered to depart in peace
with no more guarantee than his bare word.

This "peace by negotiation," though offering a
precedent which should be dear to the hearts of our
pacifists, was not to the mind of one of Jehovah's
prophets—an unnamed prophet whom later Jewish
tradition identifies with Micaiah the son of Imlah,
who figures in the sequel. Having prevailed upon a
companion to wound him, he appears before Ahab
with a blood-stained bandage on his head, and presents

his plea. According to his story, he was left in
charge of a captive on the battlefield, on the understanding that, if the man escaped, his own life was to
be forfeit. As he turned this way and that to watch
the conflict the captive slipped off. He leaves his
case to Ahab's decision, and the king can only reply,
" So shall thy judgment be : thou thyself hast decided
it."

The prophet's purpose is gained. Like the prophet
Nathan condemning the sin of David, he has made
Ahab pass sentence on himself. Tearing the bandage
from his head, he stands revealed as a prophet, and
announces the oracle of Jehovah : " Thus saith Jehovah,
Because thou hast let go out of thy hand the man
whom I had devoted to destruction, therefore thy life
shall go for his life, and thy people for his people."
" The King of Israel," we are told, " went to his house
displeased and gloomy, and returned to Samaria."

Then followed a peace of two or three years between
Israel and Syria, in the course of which, as we learn
from an Assyrian inscription, Ahab was drawn by
Ben-Hadad into an alliance against Shalmaneser III.,
king of Assyria, and sent a contingent of 2000
chariots and 10,000 foot-soldiers to the army of allies
mustered by Ben-Hadad to meet the Assyrians at
Karkar in northern Syria, in the year 854 B.C. The
issue of the battle appears to have been indecisive.
The Assyrian was checked for the time being, but at
heavy cost to the allies. It was probably in the same
year that Ahab resolved, in concert with Jehoshaphat,

king of Judah, who was perhaps his vassal, to recover from Ben-Hadad the city of Ramoth-Gilead, which the Syrian king had *not* restored in accordance with his compact.

We read last Sunday morning about the battle of Ramoth-Gilead and the death of Ahab, as related in 1 Kings xxii. The following fifty years or so was a period of heavy calamity for Israel at the hands of Ben-Hadad and his successor Hazael, and proved to the full how ill-advised Ahab had been in concluding a peace by negotiation, and without security, with a cruel and treacherous foe, and in not putting it out of his power to make further aggressions against Israel.

This chapter of ancient history carries on its surface a moral for the present time, which it is superfluous to reinforce. Ahab won his war with Syria, and then lost the peace. The issue of the present conflict would have interested the prophets of Israel no less than the struggle between Israel and Syria, since we, like them, profess to have at heart, not material gain and aggrandizement, but the cause of righteousness—the very existence, we may say, of the ideal of justice and humanity.

We are likely, if events, as we have every reason to hope, continue to take a prosperous course for the allies, to hear much in the near future of *our brother* Ben-Hadad. Let us not, like Ahab, be cajoled into trifling with the fruits of victory, and losing our peace. " Thus saith the Lord, Because thou hast let go out of thy hand the man whom I had devoted to destruction, therefore thy life shall go for his life, and thy people for his people."

We are fighting, not to destroy the German people, but to destroy Prussian militarism, root and branch. If that be scotched merely, and not killed outright, then the prophet's words, we need make no doubt, will come as true for us and for our children as they did for Ahab, and the thing which has brought a curse and a blight upon the world for the past four years will spring again from its stock, and fill the face of the world with ruin and calamity.

God grant that we may be wise in time, and not lose, through our own weakness and irresolution, the fruits of victory for which so many of our best and noblest have laid down their lives.

VI.

THE CHRISTIAN INTERPRETATION OF MESSIANIC PROPHECY.

"And He said unto them, O foolish men, and slow of heart to believe in all that the prophets have spoken! Behoved it not the Christ to suffer these things, and to enter into His glory! And beginning from Moses and from all the prophets, He interpreted to them in all the scriptures the things concerning Himself."—St. Luke xxiv. 25-27.

THE founder of this sermon [1] decreed that it should deal with "the application of the prophecies in Holy Scripture respecting the Messiah to our Lord and Saviour Jesus Christ, with an especial view to confute the arguments of Jewish commentators and to promote the Conversion to Christianity of the ancient people of God." The wording of the statute admits of some liberty in its interpretation. It is open to a preacher to address his attention mainly to the Jewish commentators, and to follow the negative course of attempting to show the inadequacy of their interpretations of Messianic prophecy. Or he may adopt the positive argument, and, taking his stand in the new light which has been shed upon the Old

[1] Dr. McBride, Principal of Magdalen Hall, Oxford,

Testament through application of historical methods of study, may trace in outline the development in Israel's religion of the great ideas which are characterized as Messianic, weighing their significance in view of the historical circumstances which gave them birth, and observing how they are drawn together and receive their full unification and satisfaction in the Person and Work of our Lord.

This latter course appears to be more in accordance with the spirit of the founder's intention than the former. Examination of the arguments of the Jewish commentators, to be complete, ought to deal with the Jewish controversy from the Christian era down to the present day—an undertaking which might well fill volumes, and which when achieved would possess but little evidential value for Christianity, and would be of interest only to a narrow circle of historical specialists. For, with the growth of knowledge and improvement of method in the various departments of Old Testament study which was witnessed by the last century, the argument from prophecy has come in a large measure to be restated, less stress is laid upon particular proof-passages and more upon the general drift of prophecy as a whole, and many of the arguments adduced in past ages by Jews and Christians, and depending upon particular interpretations, would now seem puerile, and have in the course of years died a natural death.

At the same time, altogether to ignore the Jewish arguments can scarcely be claimed to be in accordance with the design of the founder. What, I take it, the preacher is called upon to do is to look for the great outstanding objections which the Jews in all ages have advanced against the Christian application of prophecy, and briefly (as must needs be) to indicate the drift of their arguments before advancing to a consideration of the Messianic ideal, as it may be viewed in the light of modern study of the Old Testament Scriptures.

JEWISH OBJECTIONS TO THE CHRISTIAN APPLICATION OF MESSIANIC PROPHECY.

Such outstanding objections appear to fall under two heads :

1. Objection to the Christian claim that the Messiah is conceived in the Old Testament as a Person divine as well as human ; and
2. The offence of the Cross ; objection, that is to say, to the view that the Messiah is foreshadowed as destined to suffer and die for the sins of the world, and that by the most shameful of deaths.

1. We know from the Gospels that it was our Lord's claim to Divinity rather than His claim to the Messiahship which scandalized the Rabbinic authorities of His time and provoked their violent animosity. Yet our Lord Himself points out that, according to their own current canons of interpretation, the Messiah is spoken of in the Old Testament in

language which could never be satisfied by a merely human descendant of the line of David. " If then David in the spirit calls him Lord," says the great Teacher, with reference to the opening words of the cxth Psalm, " how is he his son ? " (St. Matt. xxii. 41 ff.). The argument is in form thoroughly Rabbinic. Our Lord is speaking as a Jew to Jews, and forcing them, as it were out of their own mouths, to a conclusion, which by their silence they unwillingly admit. To suppose that the incident binds us down to a particular view as to the authorship of the Psalm, involves a misconception of the conditions under which the words were spoken. Yet the conclusion, as it is inferred from Messianic prophecy as a whole, is one which the historical study of the Old Testament records has perhaps served to bring into greater prominence than before.

It would be out of place to enter at length into the Jewish arguments which have been advanced against the Christian contention that the picture of the Messiah as portrayed in the Old Testament represents Him as endowed with the divine attributes. In the main they follow a course of reasoning which has close points of contact with the arguments of Arius and his followers. As an illustration I may quote a passage from the mediæval Rabbi David Kimchi, in his commentary on the 2nd Psalm.

" The Nazarenes," he says, " interpret the Psalm of Jesus, but the verse which they cite as a proof and use as a support of their error happens to be a

stumbling-block to them. This verse is, 'Jehovah
said to Me, Thou art My Son.' For if they say to
you, He was the Son of God, reply to them that it is
not proper to use the expression 'Son of God' of
flesh and blood. For a son is of the species of his
father. Thus it would not be proper to say, 'This
horse is the son of Reuben.' If this be so, he to
whom Jehovah said, 'Thou art My Son,' must
necessarily be of His species, and be God like Him.
And, moreover, He says, 'This day have I begotten
Thee'; and he who is begotten is of the same species
as he who begets him. Say, moreover, to them that
the expression 'Father and Son' is inappropriate to
the Divine. For the Divine cannot be divided; for
it is not corporeal that it should be divided. But
God is one as regards all aspects of unity; He cannot
be multiplied nor diminished nor parted asunder.
And, moreover, say to them, A father is prior to a son
in time, and from the strength of the father does the
son proceed. And although the one term is inappropriate without the other as regards nomenclature,
for a man is not called a father until he has a son,
nor is he called a son if he has no father, yet in any
case he who is called a father when he has a son is
prior in time without doubt.

"If this be so, as regards the God whom you
speak of and describe as Father, Son, and Holy Spirit
—the part which you call Father must be prior to
the other part which you call Son. For if at all
times the two of them had been as one, they would

5

have been called twin-brethren, and you would not call them Father and Son, nor begetter and begotten. For the begetter is prior to the begotten, without doubt. And if they say that it is not proper to use the expression 'Son of God' of anything which is not of the divine species, reply to them that we are not able to speak of God (blessed be He) except in the way of metaphor, as it is said of Him, 'the mouth of Jehovah,' 'the eyes of Jehovah,' 'the ears of Jehovah,' and similar expressions; yet it is understood that this is nothing but metaphor. And so it is by way of metaphor that such expressions are used as 'Son of God,' 'Sons of God.' For whosoever performs His commandments and His commission is called 'Son,' just as a son performs the command of his father. Therefore the stars are called 'Sons of God,' as in the passage, 'and all the Sons of God shouted for joy.' So in the case of man, on account of the higher spirit which is in him, when man performs the command of God because of the wise inspiration which instructs him, God calls him 'Son.' And therefore He says, 'Thou art My Son; this day have I begotten Thee.'"

We notice at once the remarkable inconsistency of the writer. He repudiates the use of metaphor when arguing against the Christians, yet he relies upon it when offering his own explanation of the passage. The divine mystery of the eternal generation of the Son is discussed as though the terms were used not in a metaphorical but in a crude and fleshly sense; yet at the same time Kimchi claims that there *is* a metaphorical sense in which divine Sonship can be predicated of mankind.

2. We must pass on to the second objection to which I have referred—that, namely, which is aimed against the Christian claim that the Old Testament fore-shadows the advent of a suffering Redeemer who is to die for the sins of the world, and that this foreshadow-ing was fulfilled in all essentials by our Lord.

It is doubtful how far the Jews of our Lord's day interpreted the passages in the latter part of Isaiah which speak of the righteous Servant of Jehovah as having reference to a personal Redeemer who was to be identified with the Messiah. The Apostles' use of παῖς, with reference to our Lord, in such phrases as "God hath glorified *His Servant* Jesus," "God having raised up *His Servant*, hath sent Him to bless you" (Acts iii. 13–26 ; cf. iv. 30), makes it plain that they, in their enlightenment, were dwelling upon the Isaianic conception, and suggests the infer-ence that the use of the term "Servant" in a Messianic sense would not be misunderstood by their hearers. But how foreign the idea of a suffering *Messiah* was to the Jewish thought of the time is evident from the failure of our Lord's immediate followers to realize that their Master was destined to suffer, and that His Crucifixion was anything else than the death-blow to their expectations. "But we hoped that it was He which should redeem Israel," said Cleophas to the unknown wayfarer, when he had told him of the death of the prophet, Jesus of Nazareth; and he needed the reproof, "Behoved it not the Messiah to suffer these things?" and the interpretation of Scripture which followed, before he was able to realize that this was in truth a great aspect of the Messiah's work as contemplated in the Old Testament (St. Luke xxiv. 13 ff.). In the same way, we find St. Paul at Thessalonica "opening and alleging" to the Jews "from the Scriptures" "that it behoved the Messiah to suffer and to rise again from the dead," it being necessary to make them understand this before he was able to continue, "This Jesus, whom I proclaim unto you, is the Messiah" (Acts xvii. 3). It is in accordance with this Jewish standpoint that the Targum of Jonathan paraphrases the latter verses of Isa. lii. as referring to the Messiah— "Behold My servant Messiah shall prosper," but then interprets the statements of ch. liii. which relate the sufferings and death of the Servant as alluding to the nation of Israel at large. The earliest admission of belief in a suffering Messiah in the mouth of a Jew by religion appears to be that of Trypho, Justin's friendly opponent. "That the Scriptures," he says, "do state that Messiah should suffer, is plain; but we wish to learn if you have any means of proving also that it should be by a kind of suffering which is cursed in the law."[1] This passage, however, can scarcely be cited as proving that

[1] *Dialogue with Trypho*, ch. 89.

this belief was general among the Jews in the 2nd century, since it may well be that Trypho, liberal-minded and open to conviction as he clearly was, was ready to admit so much in deference to the arguments of the Christians.

In later times there grew up among the Jews the expectation of two distinct Messiahs, the Messiah ben-David and the Messiah ben-Joseph.[1] The Messiah ben-Joseph, who was first to appear, was expected to have but a short career, and to fall fighting before the gates of Jerusalem against Armilus, the representative of the heathen world-power. The Messiah ben-David was then to assume the rôle of a victorious prince, vanquishing Armilus, and subsequently raising the Messiah ben-Joseph from the dead. Whether the idea of the Messiah ben-Joseph was suggested by the figure of the suffering Servant is doubtful. His death and resurrection offer a super-ficial resemblance, but there seems to have been no suggestion that he would bear the sins of his people or that his death would be in any way vicarious. More probably the tradition, in so far as it can be said to have any Biblical connexion, is dependent upon the passage in Zech. xii. which describes the stress and deliverance of Jerusalem, and contains the obscure allusion, "They shall look on me (or, as a variant reading has it, 'him') whom they have pierced."

The great commentators Rashi, Ibn Ezra, and

[1] The earliest reference appears to be *Sukkah*, 52a, b.

David Kimchi, all explained the figure of the suffering Servant in Isaiah as referring to the nation of Israel in exile; and they seem largely to have fixed this interpretation for later times, for the exceptions to it are few and unimportant. Naturally, when the expected King-Messiah was thought of as a merely human descendant of David, it was found impossible to invest him with the attributes of the righteous Sufferer, yielding his soul as a guilt-offering for the sins of mankind.

The objections, from this Jewish standpoint, to interpreting Isa. liii. in a Messianic sense, are well voiced by Abarbanel in his commentary on the passage. " As regards," he says, " the course taken by Jonathan and our other wise men who interpret it of Messiah our righteousness, I do not know whether they mean by this Messiah ben-Joseph, who they believe is to come at the beginning of the deliverance, or whether they intend thereby Messiah ben-David, who is to come afterwards. In either case, however, the simple sense of the words will not admit of such an interpretation. Of Messiah ben-Joseph, who is to die at the outset of his career and his battles, it could not be said that he would be ' high and exalted and lofty exceedingly '; such dignity as this he could not acquire, still less maintain. Moreover, the passage says : ' His countenance was marred more than any man, he was despised and rejected of men, a man of sorrows, and acquainted with grief '; yet all this forms no part of the description of this

Messiah as given by our Rabbis; why indeed should it ? It is said, moreover : ' And with the rich in his death,' the meaning of which is not to be ascertained. And how could it be said of him that ' he shall see his seed, he shall prolong his days,' if he is to die at the outset of his career ? If, however, they interpret the prophecy of Messiah ben-David, then a difficulty arises from the words, ' His countenance was marred more than any man, and his form more than the sons of men ; he hath no form nor comeliness ' ; for Isaiah himself said [on the contrary] : ' Behold my servant whom I uphold, mine elect in whom my soul delighteth, I do put my spirit upon him ' ; and in another passage he called him ' a rod out of the stock of Jesse,' and said : ' The spirit of Jehovah shall rest upon him . . . unto him shall nations resort,' so far from his being ' despised and rejected of men, a man of sorrows, and acquainted with grief.' And, moreover, how could it be said of him, ' Surely he hath borne our sicknesses, and carried our sorrows ; yet did we esteem him stricken, smitten of God, and afflicted ' ? For he is to be a righteous king, and he is not to be stricken and smitten, but righteous and victorious. And if this be so, how can it be said of him that ' by his stripes we are healed,' and ' Jehovah hath laid on him the iniquity of us all,' and what sense can we attach to the rest of the verses which teach that he shall undergo sufferings and death for the sake of Israel ? "

All this, it must be admitted, is very sound reasoning from such premises as the Jewish standpoint allows.

I may conclude this necessarily imperfect sketch of Jewish thought with regard to the conception of a suffering Messiah by citation of two passages from the article on "Jesus of Nazareth" in the new *Jewish Encyclopædia.* "There appears," says the author, " to be no evidence of any Jewish conception of a Messiah suffering through and for his people, though there possibly was a conception of one suffering together with his people." [1]   And again, with reference to our Lord's Messianic claims in view of His Crucifixion : "The very form of his punishment would disprove those claims in Jewish eyes.   No Messiah that Jews could recognize could suffer such a death ; for he that is hanged is accursed of God (Deut. xxi. 23), ' an insult to God' (Targum, Rashi)." [2]   Turning to the article " Messiah " by another writer in the same Encyclopædia, we find no expression of any Messianic expectation for the future—surely a miserable outcome of aspirations once so lofty and inspiring !

Growth of the Messianic Expectation in the Old Testament.

Let us now turn briefly to consider the nature and characteristics of the Messianic expectation in the Old Testament.   We shall view it, as far as may be, *historically*, that is to say, in relation to the cir-

[1] Vol. vii. p. 163.   [2] *Ibid.* p. 166.

cumstances which gave it birth, and as the development of great ideas gradually worked out in history, and advancing from small beginnings towards their climax.

The earliest literature of Israel represents the relationship between Jehovah and His people under the terms of a covenant. This covenant is pictured in the old narrative as concluded between Jehovah and Abraham, the idealized founder of the nation. Thus entered upon, it is again ratified to Abraham's immediate descendants, Isaac and Jacob; and, once more, it is established at Horeb between Jehovah and the tribes of Israel, after Jehovah had marked them out as the people of His special possession through the signal deliverance from Egypt.

Now a covenant depends for its validity upon the fulfilment by both parties of the terms of agreement. But inasmuch as Jehovah's covenant was concluded once for all with Abraham, the faithful founder of the race, it is independent of the manner in which any particular generation of the children of Israel may fulfil their obligation. Failure and shortcoming in this respect might, and indeed must, involve punishment even so severe as the final cutting off of the offender from the covenant and his forfeiture of its privileges. And such a defection upon the part of Israel might be so widespread as to include the greater portion of the nation, who might fall away and for ever perish out of the covenant-relation. But that *the whole* of the nation should thus prove unfaithful was, under the terms of the covenant, regarded as impossible. Jehovah could not prove Himself untrue to the oath which He sware to Abraham. In the darkest days of apostasy an Elijah may think that he stands alone as a faithful adherent to the covenant: "The children of Israel have profaned Thy covenant, thrown down Thine altars, and slain Thy prophets with the sword, and I only am left"; yet Jehovah knows of "seven thousand in Israel, every knee which hath not bowed unto Baal, and every mouth which hath not kissed him" (1 Kings xix. 10 ff.). And whenever and wherever these faithful few are found, *they* are the true Israel with whom the covenant stands fast, and upon whom the hope of the nation is centred. Jehovah, in thus maintaining the relation, is jealous for the honour of His name. In Samuel's words, "Jehovah will not cast off His people, for His great name's sake, because it hath pleased Jehovah to make you a people unto Himself" (1 Sam. xii. 22).

Again, we have to notice Jehovah's promise to David. The ideal of the theocratic king is most nearly represented by David, whom Jehovah, by the mouth of His prophet, characterizes as "a man after His own heart" (1 Sam. xiii. 14). For David, with all his shortcomings, always recognizes the sacred trust which has been committed to him as king over Jehovah's heritage, and realizes, in the main, that condition of dependence and reliance upon the divine Ruler which should be characteristic of the human ruler in the theocratic State. Thus David is promised that he shall for ever possess "a lamp before

Jehovah at Jerusalem " (cf. 1 Kings xi. 36, xv. 4 ;
2 Kings viii. 19 ; Ps. cxxxii. 17), the quenchless
flame being emblematic of an unfailing posterity to sit
upon his throne.

It is these two ideas — the indestructibility of
Israel as a nation and of the Davidic dynasty—which
are taken up by the writing prophets of the 8th
century and later, and upon which they base their
conceptions of the Messianic Ruler and His kingdom.

In the earliest of these prophets, Amos and Hosea,
the Messianic idea is scarcely developed, and such
allusions as may be found are debatable. I will
therefore pass to Isaiah, who flourished a few years
later in the Southern kingdom.

The latter part of the 8th century B.C. was a
period of great catastrophe and change for the small
kingdoms clustered on the east of the Mediterranean.
Assyria, which had for long been the dominant force
in Western Asia, was now reaching the zenith of her
power, and the time was approaching when she
must try conclusions with Egypt, the only rival which
was likely to offer serious opposition to her victorious
career. What was to be the policy of the small
States which lay along the line of advance, and whose
existence would surely be threatened in the inevitable
conflict ? Worldly wisdom suggested the playing off
of one great power against the other, with a narrow
scrutiny of the turn which events were likely to take,
and crafty contrivance to be always on the winning
side. This, however, was not the policy of Isaiah.

He recommended a policy of isolation, in reliance upon Jehovah. Secure in her mountain-fastnesses, the little kingdom of Judah might behold the stream of conflict pass by and remain unscathed. In quietness and in confidence was to be her strength. It is with these historical circumstances that Isaiah's Messianic ideals are intimately bound up, and they form an integral part of his policy as a whole, being, in fact, its guiding principle and its justification.

Isaiah's Immanuel-prophecy, with its sequel (chs. vii., viii. 1–ix. 7), may be regarded as the most important of his Messianic utterances. There can be little doubt that Immanuel, the "sign" which the prophet offers to King Ahaz, is an idealized Messianic Person who is to be at once the symbol and the embodiment of the coming deliverance of Judah ;— "God is with us."

There has been an immense amount of controversy as to the meaning and nature of this sign. The rendering of our A.V., which represents Immanuel's mother as a virgin, follows the Septuagint, which is the source of the quotation in the first chapter of St. Matthew's Gospel. But the fact was very early recognized that the Hebrew term which is employed is not the one which would normally be selected to denote an unmarried woman, but one which simply denotes a young woman of marriageable age, without indicating whether she is married or single. Hence we find that the Greek translators Aquila, Symmachus, and Theodotion, who lived during the early days of

Jewish and Christian controversy, abandoned the LXX rendering παρθένος in favour of the more strictly accurate νεᾶνις. Upon the basis of this rendering it has been sought to deny the Messianic significance of Immanuel, and to generalize the "sign": Any young woman of an age to become a mother may name her first-born son Immanuel in view of the near approach of the deliverance of Judah from her foes.

But to a sympathetic student of the prophecy such a view is inconceivable. Immanuel is a definitely pictured individual. The land of Judah is spoken of as his land. And what are we to make of the extraordinary enthusiasm of hope with which the mere mention of his name inspires the prophet? For, after describing how the devastating wave of Assyrian invasion will sweep across the kingdom of Israel until it reaches the land of Immanuel, he suddenly breaks into the triumphant defiance :

"Take notice, all ye peoples,
And give ear, ye far countries,
Gird yourselves and be broken in pieces;
Gird yourselves and be broken in pieces.
Take counsel together, only that it may be frustrated,
Speak a word, and it shall not stand ;
For God is with us."[1]

It may be assumed, then, that the conception of Immanuel is identical with that of the Messianic

[1] Isa. viii. 9, 10. The first line is emended in accordance with the Greek version.

child of David's line of whose advent the prophet speaks later on.

Nor is it easy to believe that the last word has been said when it is stated that Immanuel's mother is described as a young woman simply and not as a virgin. For clearly there is to be something miraculous in the mere event of the child's birth. No limits are set upon the sign which Ahaz is invited to ask. He may make it deep as Sheol, or high as the heaven above. As a recent writer has ably shown, there are parallels for the idea of virgin-birth which may well have influenced popular thought in Judah at the time ;[1] and the rendering of the Septuagint translator is difficult to explain, except on the hypothesis that this was the import of the passage which was current among the Jews at least in his age. It may be noticed that there is probably an allusion to this prophecy in the words of the contemporary prophet Micah, who, after predicting the advent of an ideal ruler of David's line who is to inaugurate a new epoch, states that Jehovah will deliver the nation into the hands of its foes " until the time that she which travaileth hath brought forth " (Mic. v. 3). In a prophecy which forms the sequel to the Immanuel-prophecy (Isa. viii.-ix. 7), Isaiah further describes the Messianic ruler and his kingdom. He is invested with attributes which partake of the divine. In his

---

[1] Cf. Jeremias, *Babylonisches im Neuen Testament*, 46 ff. Since the writing of this sermon, the subject has been treated by the present writer in *Journal of Theological Studies*, July 1909, p. 580 ff.

fourfold name we may notice the titles " Wonder of a counsellor " which depicts a skill in statesmanship which is superhuman, and " God-mighty one," a title elsewhere applied only to Jehovah Himself.[1] The guiding principles of his rule are to be justice and righteousness, and he is to inaugurate a reign of peace which is to last for ever.

Another prophecy, uttered some years later at a time of great national stress, draws a still more detailed picture of the Messianic king (Isa. xi. 1–10). He is to be of the stock of Jesse, endowed with the spirit of Jehovah so as to be full of superhuman wisdom. Emphasis is again laid upon his moral characteristics, righteousness and faithfulness or steadfastness. These he will exercise for the benefit of the poor and weak, and for the stern repression of evil-doers. Thus he opens an ideal age of universal peace, in which the earth is filled with the knowledge of Jehovah as the waters cover the sea.

Time would fail were I to attempt to show even in bare outline how the same ideal is taken up and worked out by later prophets. I can only notice in passing that for Jeremiah the King's name denotes " Jehovah is our righteousness " (Jer. xxiii. 6), this indicating that he is to be the embodiment of the

---

[1] The force of this name as implying superhuman attributes remains substantially unaltered even if it be explained (as in the Jewish Revised Version, 1917), "Wonderful in counsel is God the Mighty, the Everlasting Father, the Ruler of peace." For clearly the Messiah is to be, not merely the pledge, but in a real sense the embodiment, of God's character as thus defined.

theocratic ideal, deriving his commission and the power to execute it from Jehovah as the source of grace. And, as with Isaiah, it is the moral and spiritual basis of this ruler's kingdom which rivets the prophet's vision : " This is the covenant which I will make with the house of Israel after those days, saith Jehovah, I will put My law in their inward parts, and in their heart will I write it; and I will be their God, and they shall be My people : and they shall teach no more every man his neighbour and every man his brother, saying, Know Jehovah ; for they shall all know Me, from the least of them unto the greatest of them, saith Jehovah : for I will forgive their iniquity, and their sin will I remember no more " (Jer. xxxi. 34).

It cannot, I think, too strongly be emphasized that this conception of the ideal Davidic ruler and his kingdom is not the outcome of national pride and vainglory. Those who were guided to frame it were not the kind of men so to be influenced. So far from being time-servers and men-pleasers, they constantly found themselves set in sharpest antagonism to the spirit of their age. So far from being deceived as to the present condition of their nation, they were those in whom the sense of sin and its heinousness and the need of redemption and purification were most keenly felt. They unite in predicting that the nation must pass through a period of chastisement and trial, that the gold must be separated from the dross and purified seven times in the fire, before the advent of that ideal age upon which they set their hope. And the kingdom which they foresee is no mere worldly power founded upon the force of arms. Its characteristics are moral and spiritual. In the widest conception of it, it is to be coextensive with the world; but nations flock into it because they realize that Israel's God is the only true God, and that only with Him is there righteousness and strength.

If we turn to the conception of the righteous Servant of Jehovah, of which I spoke when dealing with the Jewish interpretation of prophecy, we shall find that this also does not stand in isolation, but is the culmination of a great idea which belongs peculiarly to the genius of Israel, and which may be traced in its working from the beginning of the national life. I mean the idea that a man can feel that he stands in such a moral relation to God that he is able to commit the whole guidance of his life to Him, to feel that he is an instrument in God's hand for the performance of His good purpose, that each and all of his actions are not too trivial to come within the range of this all-embracing relation, and, in so doing, to be directed, inspired, heightened, and purified.

We may trace the working out of this idea, in a greater or less degree, in all or nearly all the outstanding characters of the Old Testament. We may trace it in Abraham, the founder of the chosen nation, leaving his country at the divine call and sojourning in a strange land, setting his faith in the promise that

6

he is to become a mighty nation, and that all the nations of the world will bless themselves in him; in Jacob, who, in spite of the twist in his character and his many failures, is able at the close of his life to speak of " the God who tended me all my life long unto this day, the angel who redeemed me from all evil "; in Joseph, who in his hour of temptation is true to his inspiration : " How can I do this great wickedness, and sin against God ? " in Moses, who, for the furtherance of a great ideal, chose " rather to be evil entreated with the people of God, than to enjoy the pleasures of sin for a season."

We may trace the same idea worked out most markedly in the lives of the prophets, whose ex-pression, " As the Lord of hosts liveth, *before whom I stand* "—*i.e.* Whose servant I am, ready to perform His bidding, lead it where it may—sums up in one brief formula their relationship to Jehovah. Thus it is that we find the title " Servant of Jehovah " used here and there throughout the Old Testament to express this special relationship. Taken up by the author of the great section in the Book of Isaiah which begins with ch. xl., it is applied in the first place to Israel as a body entrusted with a mission to the world at large. Then, as it comes home to the writer how far Israel as a whole is from answering to his ideal conception, it is narrowed down to the righteous nucleus of the nation, the Israel within Israel who has a mission first of all to his own nation, and is then to carry Jehovah's salvation to the ends of the earth. Finally, the conception takes shape in the picture of the Servant in ch. liii. realizing his mission through suffering and death, yielding up his soul as a guilt-offering for the sins of the world, rising again to a glorious future in which he is to be the spiritual father of a renewed community, and the pleasure of Jehovah is to prosper in his hand.[1]

If I have at all succeeded in my object, I have shown that modern study of the Old Testament, based on critical principles, so far from explaining away the Messianic Ideal in the Old Testament, has served to trace the historical evolution of the ideas therein contained ; yet is as far as ever from explaining them as anything else than the unique preparation in religious thought for the coming of Jesus Christ in the fulness of time. For it cannot be denied that, while the Jews, on their own showing, have been and still are unable to unify the two ideas of the King-Messiah and the suffering Servant of Jehovah, our Lord drew together and fulfilled these ideas in a manner beyond all expectation.

Modern Judaism, in its most enlightened and intellectual form, is coming more and more to confess that Jesus as man realized the highest spiritual level of the Jewish religion ; and in any case the Jews are bound to admit that it is without parallel that one

---

[1] See, further, on the conception of the ideal Servant, Sermon No. XII, p. 145.

who suffered the most shameful of deaths, " whose
visage was more marred than any man's and His form
than the sons of men," should have become the
founder of a spiritual kingdom which has resisted the
vicissitudes of time, and stands to-day as *the* great
living force in the world.

It is true, as they contend, that this kingdom has
not yet realized that world-wide dominion of which
the prophets spoke. As the writer of the Epistle
to the Hebrews says (Heb. ii. 8, 9), " We see not yet
all things put under Him." " *But*," he goes on to add,
" *we see Jesus* "; and it is upon this fact that we take
our stand ; for it is in Him that myriads claim to
have found the highest aspirations of the human
heart after holiness, peace, and joy.

A modern Jew, writing of Jesus of Nazareth, finds
occasion to remark : " No human individual, however
great in his own environment, can, according to the
Jewish view, present a perfect ideal of humanity for
all ages and phases of life. ' None is holy but God ' ;
to this Jewish conception of man Jesus also gave
expression (Matt. xix. 17). Man as the image of God
requires all the ages and historical conditions of
progress to unfold the infinite possibilities of the divine
life planted in him. ' Each age has its own types of
righteousness ' (Tanḥuma, Miḳez, Vienna ed., p. 48),
and only by the blending of all human efforts towards
the realization of the true, the good, and the beautiful
can the highest perfection be attained at the end of
history, ' each mount of vision forming a stepping

stone to Zion as the sublime goal' (Midrash Tehillim to Ps. xxxvi. 6)." [1]

No *human* individual, we grant, can fulfil such an ideal; but we claim to have the test of experience that Jesus of Nazareth, divine as well as human, has satisfied and still can satisfy the highest spiritual ideal of every age and every race. And it is on this fact that we base our sure confidence that the time will come when "the kingdoms of this world [and among them the Jewish race as a whole] shall have become the kingdoms of our Lord and of His Christ, and He shall reign for ever and ever" (Rev. xi. 15).

[1] *Jewish Enc.*, art. "Christianity," vol. iv.

VII.

REPENTANCE AND HOPE.

"Come, and let us return unto the Lord :
For He hath torn, and He will heal us ;
He hath smitten, and He will bind us up.
After two days He will revive us :
On the third day He will raise us up,
And we shall live before Him.
And let us know, let us follow on to know the Lord ;
His going forth is sure as the morning :
And He shall come unto us as the rain,
As the latter rain that watereth the earth.—Hos. vi. 1-3.

  .   .   .   .

I will heal their backsliding,
I will love them freely :
For mine anger is turned away from them.—xiv. 4.

  .   .   .   .

Who is wise, and he shall understand these things?
Prudent, and he shall know them?
For the ways of the Lord are right,
And the just shall walk in them ;
But transgressors shall fall therein."—xiv. 9.

WE are looking forward to, and, it may be, making
some attempt to prepare ourselves for, the
National Mission of Repentance and Hope. These
two words—Repentance and Hope—may be said to
summarize the message which the Hebrew prophets of
Old Testament times had for their nation ; and so it

seems to me to be appropriate that, on the Sunday mornings when it is my turn to preach, during this month and the next, I should take certain of the prophets and let them speak to you, endeavouring to draw out the import of their message, and to emphasize its value as applied to the circumstances of the present day.

Repentance, as the expression is used in the Hebrew of the Old Testament, means *return*. It is *the return* of the nation, or of the individual soul, *to God; the turning away from sin,* whether that sin be in the form of the worship of idols, or of moral wickedness and corruption. *Hope* is the hope for a new age, a renewed humanity, God's kingdom to be set up on earth.

The Hebrew prophets who have left written records of their preaching and teaching—the *writing prophets* as they are often called in distinction from earlier prophets such as Samuel and Elijah who have left no book of written teaching behind them—date from the 8th century B.C. and onwards. The earliest group of them belongs to the middle and latter part of the 8th century ; and of these two, namely, Amos and Hosea, laboured in the Northern kingdom of Israel, and two, namely, Isaiah and Micah, in the kingdom of Judah. I hope to speak, in successive sermons, of the teaching of both Amos and Hosea ; and, according to strict chronological arrangement, Amos should be taken first, since his ministry seems to have begun about ten or fifteen years earlier than that of Hosea. I have preferred, however, to place Hosea first, because it is he who strikes the keynote to which, for us as Christians, every call to repentance should be attuned—the keynote of *the love of God*.

The 8th century B.C. was, for the kingdom of Israel, a period of crisis. The latter half of the preceding century had witnessed the overrunning and raiding of the northern districts of the land of Israel by the country's hereditary foe, the Syrians of Damascus under Hazael. The tide of Israel's fortunes turned under Joash, the grandson of Jehu, whose accession nearly synchronized with the beginning of the new century (it is to be placed about 798 B.C.). You will remember the vivid story in 2 Kings xiii. of the young king's visit to the prophet Elisha as he lay on his death-bed—how the aged prophet made him shoot an arrow out of the window eastward, placing his hands upon the king's hands as he drew the bow, and then uttering the oracle :

> "Jehovah's arrow of victory,
> Even the arrow of victory over Syria:
> For thou shalt smite the Syrians in Aphek,
> Till thou have consumed them"—

an oracle which was fulfilled in the three decisive victories which Joash gained against the Syrians, by which he recovered the cities of Israel which had been lost under his predecessors.

Joash was succeeded on the throne of Israel by King Jeroboam II., whose long reign of forty-one years lasted from about 782 to 741 B.C. Jeroboam II. continued

Israel's victorious career, and indeed proved himself
the most successful king Israel had known since the
days of the division of the kingdom after the death
of Solomon.   Success in battle inaugurated a long
period of peace and material prosperity; and it is
during this period that we must place the beginning of the prophetic ministries of both Amos and
Hosea.

If we look outside the Old Testament and study
the Assyrian inscriptions, we are able to discern very
clearly the external causes which contributed to this
change in Israel's fortunes.   Beyond the borders of
the Syrian kingdom of Damascus to the N.E. there
lay the kingdom of Assyria, at that time by far the
most powerful factor in the politics of Western Asia.
Assyria had, for a century or more, been pushing
westwards, gradually wearing down the small Syrian
States, including Damascus, which barred her path in
that direction.   So long as these small western States
were content to sink their own differences, and to
offer a united front to the aggressor, they were able to
make a fair show of resistance; but, taken individually
by Assyria, their power was gradually broken and
destroyed.   We know, as a matter of fact, that Ben-
Hadad III., the king of Damascus who succeeded
Hazael the Syrian oppressor of Israel, underwent such
a staggering blow from Assyria as must practically
have crippled his military strength; and it was
doubtless owing to this that Joash of Israel was able
to gain important successes against him.   Meanwhile,

internal dissensions within the kingdom of Assyria curtailed her aggressive power for a period of forty or fifty years; and Jeroboam II., whose reign coincided with this period, was thus able to extend and consolidate the kingdom of Israel, and to raise it to the pitch of prosperity at which we find it in the time of Amos and Hosea.

But, as has so often happened in the history of nations, material prosperity brought vice and moral decadence in its train. The prophet Amos draws a lurid picture of the social conditions against which he was irresistibly moved to inveigh. The wealth of the nation had materially increased, but this wealth was far from being equally apportioned. The rich and influential became richer year by year; but their riches were amassed at the expense of the humbler classes, who were downtrodden and overburdened with cruel exactions. In a country in which the sources of wealth were, then as now, mainly agricultural, the aim of the large landowner was to increase his estates through the extinction of the peasant-proprietor; and a cruel system of usury allowed of the selling of the indigent debtor into slavery, so that Amos actually speaks of the needy being sold up for failure to find the price of a pair of shoes. At the same time, the grossest forms of vice appear to have infected all classes alike. It will be sufficient to cite Hosea's terse summary: "There is no truth, nor loving-kindness, nor knowledge of God in the land. There is nought but swearing and breaking faith, and killing, and stealing, and committing adultery; they break out, and blood toucheth blood" (Hos. iv. 1*b*, 2).

And, in spite of the successes which Israel had gained against external foes, it was, as I have already said, politically speaking, a period of crisis for the nation. To those who could read the signs of the times, Assyria, though temporarily in the background, offered an abiding menace. Given the advent of a powerful and energetic king, who could rightly organize and wield her tremendous resources, and she must be again to the fore; and this time unchecked by the Syrian buffer States which had formerly done so much to bar her westward expansion. Both Amos and Hosea foresaw that punishment would fall upon the guilty nation of Israel from this source; and the accuracy of their foresight was speedily to be proved. On the death of Jeroboam II. in or about 741 B.C., Israel was apparently at the height of her prosperity. Only seven years later (in 734) Tiglath-Pileser IV. of Assyria invaded and conquered the northern parts of the kingdom, carrying a large part of the population into captivity. Ten years later still Samaria was invested by the army of Shalmaneser V., and after standing a three years' siege fell before the Assyrians in 722, the first year of Sargon, Shalmaneser's successor. Sargon's statement in his Annals runs as follows: "Samaria I besieged and conquered; 27,290 of its inhabitants I carried captive; the rest of the people I allowed to retain their possessions; my officers as prefects I appointed over them; the

tribute of the former kings I laid upon them." Thus
the national life of the Northern kingdom of Israel
came to an end.

Let us now turn more particularly to Hosea, and
his call of the nation to repentance. The divine
message came to the prophet through the most
dreadful domestic sorrow which can fall to the lot of
man. His wife, named Gomer, proved herself
unfaithful to the marriage-relationship, finally desert-
ing him, and sinking, apparently, into the position of
a slave. Yet, in spite of all, the prophet's love for
her was so great that he would not cast her off. He
buys her back from her ignominious position and
restores her to his home, firmly but tenderly holding
her in seclusion for a time that she may be weaned
from her desire to resume her evil course, and upon
his side again plighting his troth to her that he will
never form connexion with any woman but with her
only.

Hosea's love for Gomer, strong and disciplined as
resting on a moral basis, yet at the same time infinitely
tender, suggests to him a parable of the covenant-
relation between Jehovah and the apostate Israel of
his age. His reclaiming of his wife out of her
miserable state is dictated by a love which is a
reflection of that with which "Jehovah loveth the
children of Israel" (iii. 1).

Thus the way is prepared for the representation of
the bond between Jehovah and Israel as being like

to the marriage-relationship. Israel acts unfaithfully
and must undergo the penalty; but Jehovah's love is
changeless, will never cast off, and must at last
triumph. " I will betroth thee unto Me for ever;
yea, I will betroth thee unto Me in righteousness, and
in judgment, and in loving-kindness, and in mercies.
I will even betroth thee unto Me in faithfulness : and
thou shalt know Jehovah" (ii. 19, 20). Such a
promise, however, is incapable of realization apart
from a preceding discipline of repentance and purgation.
Just as Gomer needed a long period of seclusion in
order that she might be weaned from her evil ways,
and might come to a better mind, so " the children of
Israel shall abide many days without king, and without
prince, and without sacrifice, and without pillar, and
without ephod or teraphim : afterward shall the
children of Israel return, and seek Jehovah their God,
and David their king; and shall come with fear unto
Jehovah and to His goodness in the latter days"
(iii. 4 f.).

Again, Israel is Jehovah's refractory son; yet, none
the less, the son of His love :

" When Israel was a child, then I loved him,
And called My son out of Egypt.
As I called them, so they went from Me ;
They sacrificed unto the Baals, and burned incense
to graven images.
Yet *I* taught Israel to walk ;
I took them in My arms ;
But they knew not that *I* healed them.
I drew them with cords of a man,
With bands of love" (xi. 1-4).

Here we have the tenderest picture of the little child taking his first steps, guided and assisted by the hand of his father.

In this passage, ch. xi. 4, as also in ch. iii. 1, the term employed to denote "love" is in Hebrew *ahăbha*, the ordinary word for the strongest of human affections. Elsewhere, however, throughout the prophecy we find the expression *hésedh*, which is best rendered "loving-kindness." This word, as distinct from the other, gives prominence to the moral basis upon which the divine love rests; and it is this idea which conditions the whole tone of Hosea's book.

"Loving-kindness," as viewed by Hosea, has a threefold relationship. It is, as we have noticed, the bond which unites Jehovah to Israel. It should be also the bond which unites Israel to Jehovah. And, in vital connexion with this latter, there lies the social obligation between man and man. It is loving-kindness that Jehovah desires of Israel rather than the barren performance of sacrificial ritual (vi. 6): Israel's neglect of this obligation is definitely described as a breach of the covenant-relation (vi. 7): their loving-kindness is as transient as the morning cloud, and as the dew which goeth early away (vi. 4): it is lacking altogether from the land, and, in consequence, social anarchy is rampant (iv. 1, 2). The prophet's exhortation is, "Sow to yourself in righteousness, reap according to loving-kindness; break up your fallow ground: for it is time to seek Jehovah, till He come and rain righteousness upon you" (x. 12). "Turn thou to thy God; keep loving-kindness and judgment, and wait on thy God continually " (xii. 6).

Such, in brief, is Hosea's contribution towards the call to repentance. It embodies a conception which is taken up and worked out, along one line or another, in the later literature of the Old Testament, and also, as will immediately occur to you, in our Lord's parable of the Prodigal Son. However careless we may be, in a general way, of the claims of religion, we cannot help being thrilled by the inherent beauty of that story: " While he was yet a great way off, his father saw him, and had compassion on him, and ran, and fell on his neck and kissed him. And the son said to him, Father, I have sinned against heaven, and before thee: I am no more worthy to be called thy son" (St. Luke xv. 20, 21).

Let me then, this morning, without going further, leave with you the thought of the love of God calling us to repentance. Once we grasp the conception of God as a loving Father, ready to meet half-way each feeble effort, ready to receive and to forgive, we shall not ask whether we need repentance as individuals or as a nation, we shall not doubt but that there is ample room for amendment of life, and, thank God, unfailing hope for the future.

> " Who is wise, and he shall understand these things?
> Prudent, and he shall know them?
> For the ways of the Lord are right,
> And the just shall walk in them;
> But transgressors shall fall therein."

VIII.

PRIVILEGE AND RESPONSIBILITY

"Hear this word that the Lord hath spoken against you,
O children of Israel, against the whole family which I brought
up out of the land of Egypt, saying:

You only have I known of all the families of the earth:
Therefore I will visit upon you all your iniquities."

AMOS iii. 1, 2.

AS I noticed in my sermon of a fortnight ago, the
prophet Amos, like Hosea, addressed his message
to the Northern kingdom of Israel during the reign of
Jeroboam II.—a period of great material prosperity
for Israel, which, however, was destined shortly to be
followed by calamity, and, eventually, by the downfall of the kingdom at the hands of the mighty empire
of Assyria. I gave an outline of the political circumstances of the times as an introduction to my sermon
on the message of Hosea; and it is unnecessary to go
over the same ground again. I may remind you,
however, that the prophetic career of Amos is to be
dated a little earlier than that of Hosea, beginning
probably about 760 B.C.; and that the kingdom of
Israel, though apparently at the height of its prosperity
at this time, was destined to last less than forty years

longer, its capital city, Samaria, falling before the Assyrians in 722 B.C., a large part of the population undergoing deportation to Assyria, and the land becoming thenceforward an Assyrian province administered by Assyrian officials.

Unlike Hosea, Amos was not himself a member of the kingdom of Israel, but belonged to the kingdom of Judah in the south. His native village, Tekoa, lay in the hills ten miles south of Jerusalem, upon the verge of the wilderness of Judah which stretches down towards the Dead Sea. This is a district which is perhaps more rugged and barren than any part of Palestine—and Palestine as a whole is a country which the modern tourist commonly regards as unpicturesque and disappointing: yet to my mind the hill-country of Judah possesses a certain austere attraction which is all its own.

Picture to yourselves a range of rolling limestone hills with frequent outcrops of grey rock and loose scattered stones, bare and parched enough in summer but bright in the springtime with scarlet anemones and the small pink cyclamen which nestles under the rocks. The range is almost treeless except for broken and stunted coppice a few feet high here and there, or isolated trees in more favoured situations. Away towards the east the hills become barer and more forbidding as they sink towards the Dead Sea, looking in parts very like the folds and contours of a raised pasteboard model-map tinted with greenish brown Between the hills you may obtain a glimpse of the

7

bright blue of the Dead Sea, lying some 4000 feet below you in the strange deep chasm which is gashed from north to south across the land, and which at the Dead Sea level falls nearly 1300 feet below the level of the Mediterranean. Beyond this are the hills of Moab, which kindle to a beautiful pearly pink in the afterglow of sunset. On the western portion of the range you may here and there see the hillsides cut in terraces where formerly the vine was cultivated; but farther east these traces disappear, and the country is—as it must always have been—a wild and desolate moorland, where you may ride for hours without seeing a human being except maybe a solitary shepherd with his flock, and without hearing a sound except the call of the partridge on the hillside.

Amid this scenery, then, the prophet Amos spent his life. He was not a prophet by profession: "I was no prophet, neither was I a prophet's son," he says, i.e. he had not undergone any special training in one of the prophetic schools or guilds which we find scattered about the land in the days of Elijah and Elisha. His business was the raising of a breed of sheep, stunted and ugly in appearance but highly prized on account of the quality of its wool; and this he supplemented by the cultivation of sycamore-figs, which may be grown in the more sheltered valleys of this barren district—a sweet and watery fruit which is eaten by the poorest of the Syrian peasantry.

We cannot fail to notice how the country-surroundings amidst which Amos lived have coloured his thought and language.   The roar of the lion as it springs upon its prey; the shepherd rescuing from the lion's mouth a few torn fragments of his sheep; the man fleeing in terror from a lion, only to encounter the more formidable Syrian bear; the clap-net springing up from the ground as it encloses the unwary bird; the heavy farm-waggon piled high with sheaves and blocking the narrow pathway—these are some of the symbols which the prophet uses to illustrate and enforce the lessons which he has to teach.

Yet though so thoroughly a son of the country, moving and thinking among the scenes and sounds of rural life, it is obvious that Amos was well versed in the moral and social conditions of the land of Israel as a whole, and in the outside movements in the wider political world.   This is probably to be explained by the fact that, as a wool-grower, he would from time to time have to travel in order to reach the markets of the land.   Only some four or five miles west of Tekoa he would strike the great main road running north and south through Palestine, and by this no doubt he made periodical visits to the principal cities of the Northern kingdom.   Here he would encounter the throngs of pilgrims to whom he alludes, journeying to the ancient sanctuary of Beer-sheba in the south, merchants and pedlars of every description, Phœnician traders who had dealings with the outside world, and many a casual traveller besides; and from them he would learn the news of the times, details of what was going on, and rumours of what might be expected, whether within Palestine itself or in the surrounding countries.[1]

Or, arrived at Bethel or Samaria, he would see for himself evidence of the social evils of which he speaks; the ostentatious luxury and wealth of the few, purchased through exaction and oppression practised on the many; the drunkenness and immorality; the false weights employed in buying and selling; the hasting to get rich at whatever cost.

> "When will the new moon be gone that we may sell corn?
> And the Sabbath, that we may set forth wheat?
> Making the ephah small, and the shekel great,
> And dealing falsely with balances of deceit;
> That we may buy the poor for silver,
> And the needy for a pair of shoes,
> And sell the refuse of the wheat" (viii. 5, 6).

All this, too, combined with the outward show of religion, the maintenance of temple-ritual with its costly sacrifices, the observance of feast and fast days; as though *that* alone were what Jehovah desired of His people, and *that* were sufficient to make Him regard them with a favourable eye, and accord them His blessing and support.

It was in his native wilderness that the call came to Amos to undertake his prophetic ministry. "Jehovah took me from after the sheep," he says, "and said to me, Go, prophesy unto My people

---

[1] This paragraph is based on G. A. Smith, *The Book of the Twelve Prophets*, i. 79 f. The description of Amos' country which precedes is drawn from the writer's personal knowledge of it.

Israel" (ch. vii. 15).   And, in his acceptance of the
call and interpretation of its meaning, we notice the
influence of his wilderness-life, with its constant
watchfulness, constant alertness, and simple, clear-
sighted apprehension of the relation between cause
and effect.

> " Do two men walk together,
>   Except by appointment ?
> Doth a lion roar in the forest,
>   When prey he hath none ?
> Doth a young lion utter his voice,
>   Except he have captured ?
> Doth a bird fall down to the earth,
>   Where no trap is for him ?
> Doth a clap-net spring up from the ground,
>   Without capturing ought ?
> Shall a trumpet be blown in a city,
>   And the people not tremble ?
> Shall misfortune befall a city,
>   And Jehovah have not wrought it ?
>
> ·   ·   ·   ·   ·   ·
>
> The lion hath roared : who shall not fear ?
> The Lord Jehovah hath spoken : who can but prophesy ? "
>
> (ch. iii. 3–8).

That is to say, just as to those who are accustomed
to interpret the sights and sounds of the wilderness
the unusual appearance of two men in consultation
implies that their meeting is no chance one, but that
they have come together by agreement ; just as the
sudden roar of a lion is proof positive that he has
struck down his prey, and the sight of a bird flutter-
ing up and then falling back to the ground proves
that he is held by a snare ; similarly, the sounding

of the alarum is a sure warning of impending danger, and the occurrence of calamity is a sign that Jehovah has willed it. And if the sound of the lion's roar strikes fear into the hearer's heart, on the certain knowledge that it is no mere meaningless sound but that successful hunting is afoot, so the inward voice of Jehovah as heard by the prophet is likewise no mere empty sound, but the presage of impending calamity; He has given the warning, and the prophet is bound to publish it. As the thought has been well summed up: "The prophet then is made sure of his message by the agreement between the inward convictions of his soul and the outward events of the day. When these walk together, it proves that they have come of a common purpose. He who causes the events— it is Jehovah Himself, 'for shall there be evil in a city, and Jehovah not have done it?'—must be author also of the inner voice or conviction which agrees with them. 'Who,' then, 'can but prophesy?'"[1]

There is much in the message of Amos which we might profitably consider; but for the present we must confine ourselves to a brief notice of the two main points which may be said to constitute his chief contribution to the religious thought of his times.

1. The first is the great emphasis which he lays upon the indissoluble connexion between religion and social morality. This, of course, is not altogether a new thought in the religious belief of ancient Israel; but we may safely say that never before

---

[1] G. A. Smith, *op. cit.* p. 91.

had it been stated in more cogent language, and never before proclaimed in the ears of a community which seemed more utterly oblivious—or, perhaps we should say, unconscious—of its meaning.

Let us listen to the voice of Jehovah, speaking through the burning words of His prophet:

> " I hate, I despise your feasts,
>   And I delight not in your solemn assemblies.
>   Though ye offer Me burnt-offerings
>   And your meal-offerings, I will not accept them,
>   And the peace-offerings of your fatlings I will not regard.
>   Take away from Me the noise of thy songs,
>   And the melody of thy viols I will not hear :
>   But let justice run down like water,
>   And righteousness like a perennial stream " (ch. v. 21–24).

2. Secondly—and this point stands in intimate connexion with the other—Amos is, so far as we know, the first Old Testament teacher to advance and to emphasize the full doctrine of Monotheism. Though earlier teachers, from Moses onwards, had emphasized the truth that Jehovah was Israel's only God, the doctrine does not seem to have been taught, or at any rate to have been generally understood, that He was likewise the God of the whole earth. In earlier times He seems to have been thought of rather as the *national* God, all-powerful, indeed, within His own proper sphere, and a mighty leader in battle, but standing out of relation to, and exercising no influence over, the surrounding nations, who were thought similarly to possess *their* own national deities, who exercised a similar sway over their own national

territory. Thus we find even a man like David expostulating with Saul for his unceasing persecution of him, and saying, " If it be Jehovah that hath stirred thee up against me, let Him accept an offering : but if it be the children of men, cursed be they before Jehovah ; for they have driven me out this day that I should not cleave unto the heritage of Jehovah, saying, Go, serve other gods " (1 Sam. xxvi. 19). Here the underlying thought in David's mind is that, if he is driven outside Jehovah's heritage—His land—he is thereby precluded from the worship of Jehovah. He cannot serve Jehovah in a territory which Jehovah does not occupy, over which He exercises no supervision ; but, in such a position, can only worship the god to whom the territory belongs. I might cite other passages to the like effect.[1]

It is easy to understand the influence which such a belief must have had upon the conception of Jehovah's moral demands, at any rate in the minds of the great bulk of the nation. However lofty the conception of Jehovah's character and of His ethical demands may have been in the minds of the spiritual leaders of Israel, there must always have existed, for the nation in general, the underlying comfortable conviction that, after all, the interests of the national God were bound up with those of His people, that He would, on the whole, be ready to look with a lenient eye upon their delinquencies, so long as His

---

[1] See, further, Sermon XI, p. 134.

ritual was duly performed, and His altar heaped high with acceptable sacrifices.

Upon this easy-going conception of religion and its obligations Amos breaks with a new announcement as to Jehovah's relation to the world at large. In asserting, as he does in the cycle of prophecies in his two opening chapters, that Jehovah has dealings with the surrounding nations, judging them by a moral standard, and, as it were, placing them in line with his own people, Israel and Judah, he is asserting something which comes to his hearers as a new and strange revelation. The statement that, just as Jehovah in time past brought up Israel out of Egypt, so did He also bring the Philistines from Caphtor and the Syrians from Kir (ix. 7), is a *fresh* fact, startlingly subversive of the old idea of Jehovah's relation to His people as national God. For the *special* care lavished by Jehovah upon Israel as the people of His choice implies, on Israel's part, special responsibilities. "To whomsoever much is given, of him shall much be required." Thus the keynote of the Book of Amos is found in the passage which I took as my text:

"You only have I known of all the families of the earth";

therefore—not, as might have been expected, will I mete out to you special favour, and shut my eyes to your shortcomings, but—

"Therefore will I visit upon you all your iniquities"
(ch. iii. 2).

And so, to the loose-living and easy-going magnates of the kingdom of Israel, who, secure in their limited and purblind conception of the Deity, whose favour, they confidently assume, they have ensured by their costly sacrifices and regularly-discharged ritual, *desired the Day of Jehovah,* upon the assumption that this must necessarily be a day on which their national God would lead them forth to victory over the nation's foes, Amos addresses the pertinent question:

"Wherefore do ye desire the Day of Jehovah?
It is darkness, and not light.
As if a man were to flee from a lion,
And a bear were to meet him;
Or were to go into the house, and lean his arm against
    the wall,
And a serpent were to bite him.
Is not the Day of Jehovah darkness and not light?
Even deep gloom, and no brightness in it?" (ch. v. 18–20).

Here we first have the conception of the Day of Jehovah as a great and signal Day of Judgment, on which He will vindicate His essential righteousness against all that is by nature opposed to it.

We may well pause to ask ourselves the question— How was it that this child of nature, this simple countryman who lived his life for the most part in solitude, with few companions but his sheep and the wild beasts and birds of the hillside, with no education in the prophetic schools of the time, should have hit upon a conception of God's sphere of action, of His moral demands, and of His working in the world, so lofty that no one since has been able to improve upon it, and that it appears to religious thinkers at the present day to be fundamental? Critical investigation of the growth of the Old Testament religion can offer no other answer than that here we have the direct revelation of God put into the heart of one of the simplest—and perhaps for that reason, one of the most readily receptive—of His servants. It is, in fact, the explanation which Amos himself gives, the fact that an effect implies, and indeed demands, the pre-existence of an adequate cause :

> " The Lord Jehovah hath spoken :
> Who can but prophesy ? "

I have run on for so long upon Amos and his message that I have left myself little time to apply his teaching to the events of the present day—though perhaps after all the showing of what a prophet's message was intended to convey to the men of his own time is the most effective method of applying it to ourselves, since in so doing it necessarily teaches its own lesson.

The fundamental lesson is, no doubt, that great crises in the history of nations are not causeless : they have their meaning as the visitation of Almighty God —the Day of Jehovah.

Taken in detail, it comes, perhaps, more readily to us to apply the warnings and denunciations of Amos to our adversaries than to ourselves. We may draw an excellent parallel between the old Israelite conception of Jehovah as a merely national Deity, so

keenly wrapped up in the fate of His own nation as
to wink at its shortcomings, and the German Emperor's
Gott mit uns, the German God who tolerates or favours
any method of frightfulness which may tend to the
world-wide establishment of his chosen race, and the
triumph of their *Kultur*.   Again, we can hardly fail
to observe the resemblance between the careless sin-
loving Israelite's desire for the Day of Jehovah as a
day of national victory, and the toast *Am Tag*, "To
the Day," as given and drunk by the German naval
officer; and we, for our part, live in the happy confidence that that Day, when it arrives, will be for him
darkness and not light.

But what of ourselves?   We also are suffering to
a degree to which probably we have never before
suffered as a nation.   What is the meaning of it?

We are able, thank God, to see in His chastening
hand the hand of love, drawing us to Himself, effacing
the baser metal of our national character, and bringing
out those nobler qualities which have long lain
dormant, and, it may be, even unsuspected.   This is
a side of God's dealing which is practically untouched
by Amos.   Partly, perhaps, owing to his temperament,
and partly to the fact that he was not himself a
member of the Northern kingdom, he was unable,
like Hosea, to agonize over the fate of the nation, and
to utter the message of God's changeless love calling
it back to Himself.   Here we must supplement the
teaching of the one prophet by that of the other.

There remains, however, the cardinal fact that true

Religion is vitally bound up with social morality, with purity of thought and action, temperance, just dealing between man and man, the alleviation of the misery of the poor, the repudiation of undue luxury, the striving after high ideals. If, as we hope and trust, we are in a true sense a privileged nation, we have to recollect that, as Amos teaches, special privilege involves special moral responsibility. Have we, as a nation and as individuals, realized as yet and put into practice all that is implied in this?

"Let Justice flow down like water,
And Righteousness like a perennial stream" (ch. v. 24).

That was the message which Amos had for his contemporaries; and that is the message which he hands on to us to-day.

IX

ISAIAH'S PARABLE OF THE HARVEST.

" 23 Give ye ear, and hear my voice;
    Hearken, and hear my speech.
24 Doth the ploughman plough continually,
    Opening and harrowing his land?
25 When he hath levelled its surface,
    Doth he not sow fitches broadcast,
    And scatter cummin,
    And put in wheat and barley,
    And spelt at the border thereof?
26 And he treateth each of them discreetly,
    His God teaching him.
27 For fitches are not threshed with a sledge,
    Neither is a cart-wheel turned upon cummin;
    But fitches are beaten out with a staff,
    And cummin with a rod.
28 Is bread-corn crushed?
    Nay! he will not for ever be threshing it;
    But he rolleth his cart-wheel over it,
    And separateth it without crushing it.
29 This also cometh forth from the Lord of hosts,
    Wonderful is His counsel, great is His wisdom." [1]

                          Isa. xxviii. 23–29.

---

[1] The text of this passage, as it stands in the Hebrew Bible, has undergone some small amount of corruption in places; and the rendering adopted implies such amount of emendation as is demanded by rhythm and general connexion in sense.

THIS little parable was spoken by Isaiah in time of
war—or, at any rate, when war was imminent,
and the kingdom of Judah was in a condition of
distress and anxiety. Though standing detached from
its context, it occurs in a group of prophecies which
preluded the great invasion of the Assyrian king
Sennacherib in B.C. 701, and his devastation of the
land of Judah.

For many years previously the foreign policy of
the kingdom of Judah had been torn asunder by
conflicting counsels. Some thirty-five years before
this date, in the reign of the weak King Ahaz, Judah,
of her own free will and against the urgent advice of
the prophet-statesman Isaiah, had called in the aid of
Assyria against Israel and Damascus; and, so doing,
had made herself once and for all the vassal of
Assyria, and subject to a heavy and vexatious annual
tribute.

As time went on there arose a political party in
Judah which favoured the casting off of the yoke of
Assyria, and the forming of an alliance with Egypt
upon equal terms. Here again Isaiah intervened as
leader of the opposition-party. Opposed as he had
been in the first instance to the making of an alliance
with Assyria, he now showed great political insight
in accurately assessing the relative power of Assyria
and of Egypt; and in divining that the latter, though
free enough in inciting the small kingdoms which
formed buffer States between herself and Assyria to
revolt against the latter power in reliance upon her

promises of help, yet would never be ready with effective aid when the crisis arrived.

For many years the pendulum oscillated between the policy of Isaiah and that of the Egyptian party in Judah. King Hezekiah, who had succeeded Ahaz in 727 B.C., was a good king; but—somewhat lacking in strength of character—he was apt to be swayed hither and thither by conflicting counsels. More than once the small States which lay along the Mediterranean sea-board were incited by Egypt to revolt against Assyria, with disastrous results to themselves. On each occasion Egypt failed to lend effective aid when such aid was most needed, and abandoned her dupes to their fate.

Once at least during this period (in 711 B.C.) Judah seems to have been drawn into the alliance, though not so seriously as to involve her downfall; for she appears to have escaped the invasion which devastated the land of her ally, Philistia, at the humiliating cost of a heavy war-indemnity. Such a set-back to the policy of the Egyptian party naturally strengthened the political position of Isaiah for the time being.[1]

---

[1] The attack on the Philistine city of Ashdod by Sargon's general, mentioned in Isa. xx. 1, was due to a revolt in which, as the Assyrian king tells us, Philistia, Judah, Edom, and Moab were planning sedition. The fact that, so far as we know, Judah escaped reprisals can only have been due to timely submission and the payment of an indemnity; and it may well have been the acceptance of this indemnity and the retirement of the Assyrians which caused the scenes of unseemly rejoicing pictured in Isa. xxii. 1–14, which so deeply stirred the indignation of Isaiah. It is significant that the prophecy immediately succeeding, xxii. 15 ff., deals with the degradation of Shebna from his position as grand vizier. Isaiah's antagonism

But, as years went on, the lessons of experience were forgotten, and the old position of affairs recurred. The death of the Assyrian King Sargon in 705 B.C., and the accession of his son Sennacherib, led to a ferment among the smaller kingdoms of Western Asia, and to a renewed attempt to shake themselves free from Assyria. This time, in spite of the warnings of Isaiah, Judah was seriously involved.

Sennacherib's third campaign, which took place in 701 B.C., was devoted to quelling this insurrection. After marching first to Phœnicia and defeating the King of Tyre, he received the submission of the other Phœnician cities, together with that of Ammon, Moab, and Edom, who, apparently, hastened to make terms with him without striking a blow. Sennacherib then turned his arms against Philistia, where Hezekiah of Judah seems to have assumed the suzerainty, and to have deposed the vassal-princes who remained faithful to Assyria, substituting others in their place. After quelling all opposition in this quarter, he encountered, on the southern border of Philistia, an army which had been hastily raised and dispatched to the aid of the allies by Shabaka, king of Egypt. This he utterly routed. Then, overrunning the land of Judah, he captured forty-six fortified cities together with in-

to Shebna was probably due to the fact that he was leader of the opposing political party which favoured alliance with Egypt ; and the hopeless breakdown of this policy in 711 B.C. may well have enabled Isaiah to secure Shebna's degradation and the elevation of Eliakim in his place. At the time of Sennacherib's invasion in 701 B.C. it is Eliakim who is grand vizier, while Shebna holds the inferior position of scribe or recorder (Isa, xxxvi. 3).

8

numerable open towns, and laid siege to Jerusalem, shutting up Hezekiah in his capital (so he tells us) " like a bird in a cage."

It was at this stage that Hezekiah was compelled to sue for terms, as we read in 2 Kings xviii. 14 : " And Hezekiah, king of Judah, sent to the king of Assyria to Lachish, saying, I have offended; return from me : that which thou puttest on me will I bear. And the king of Assyria appointed unto Hezekiah, king of Judah, 300 talents of silver and 30 talents of gold. And Hezekiah gave him all the silver that was found in the house of the Lord, and in the treasures of the king's house. At that time did Hezekiah cut off the gold from the doors of the temple of the Lord, and from the. pillars which Hezekiah, king of Judah, had overlaid, and gave it to the king of Assyria." The account of this heavy tribute is corroborated and enlarged upon in Sennacherib's own inscription, the original of which is extant in the British Museum. It is to this inscription that I owe such details of the campaign as are not preserved in the Old Testament narrative.

You will be familiar with what followed from the vivid narrative of the Old Testament. Sennacherib seems to have accepted the indemnity and to have concluded a treaty without demanding the capitulation of Jerusalem. Probably, as he was anxious to push on and invade Egypt, he resolved not to waste time in the reduction of a fortress which was so nearly impregnable that it could hardly be captured

by direct assault. On second thoughts, however, he
decided that it was unwise to leave so strong a
fortress untaken in his rear; so, in defiance of his
treaty-obligations, he detached a portion of his army
under a high official bearing the title of the Rabshakeh,
and demanded the unconditional surrender of Jerusalem. Hezekiah was encouraged by Isaiah to trust
in God and to hold out. When the outlook seemed
blackest, the sudden decimation of the main Assyrian
army by a pestilence (the fact of which is in-
dependently corroborated by the Greek historian
Herodotus),[1] together—as it seems—with the receipt
of news of the outbreak of a rebellion in Assyria,
compelled Sennacherib to abandon his campaign and
return to his country.

Jerusalem was saved; but at what a cost! The
condition of Judah as a whole must have been not
unlike that of Belgium at the present time; and
many years must have elapsed before the land was
able to regain its former condition.

It was times such as these which called forth
Isaiah's parable which I have taken as my text. The
parable appears to have been addressed to the
prophet's own immediate circle of adherents and
disciples; and it was designed to answer a question
which had been vexing their minds, and which we may
conjecture to have been cast in the following form:

Granted the truth of Isaiah's teaching, that Jehovah
was no mere *national* deity—such as the Assyrian

---

[1] Cf. the account of Herodotus' narrative given on p. 236.

supposed Him to be, along with the gods of Hamath and Arpad and many another country—but the God of the whole earth who holds the fate of nations in His hand and uses them as the instruments of His judgments; why should He allow events to take such a course that good and bad alike must suffer? Judah, indeed, deserved punishment for her sins; but was this punishment to take such a form as to threaten the whole nation with extinction? Were those who held fast to the standard of religion and morality as enunciated by Jehovah's prophets to be involved, in spite of all, in one common ruin?

Isaiah's parable falls into two parts. Let us examine its meaning.

The first part runs as follows.

> "Doth the ploughman plough continually,
> Opening and harrowing his land?
> When he hath levelled its surface,
> Doth he not sow fitches broadcast,
> And scatter cummin,
> And put in wheat and barley,
> And spelt as the border thereof?
> And he treateth each of them discreetly,
> His God teaching him."

The point is this. Ploughing is not an end in itself. It is not a mere blind instinct for turning over the ground which actuates the farmer. He does it *with a purpose in view*; and this purpose is *the preparation of a seed-plot*. When the ground has been thoroughly prepared—both opened up and also harrowed to break up the clods and to level the surface—then he puts in his seed; and this, again, he does in accordance with a predetermined method, sowing some seeds broadcast and planting others with a drill, acting with a wisdom which, if we trace it to its ultimate source, must be regarded as the outcome of the inspiration conferred on him by God.

In just the same way, God ploughs in order that He may sow. His judgments are not vindictive. Their end is not destruction. He is ploughing in order to prepare a seed-plot in which the work will be carried on with that divine wisdom and method which is shadowed and typified in the human wisdom with which He endows the agriculturist. This is in accordance with Isaiah's teaching elsewhere, in which he lays stress upon the existence of a holy seed within the nation—as it were, an Israel within Israel—in which all that is best in the race is to be disciplined and purified in order that it may bear abundant fruit in the future.

Let us now take the second part of the parable. It has to do with another agricultural operation—that of threshing.

> " For fitches are not threshed with a sledge,
>   Neither is a cart-wheel turned upon cummin ;
>   But fitches are beaten out with a staff,
>   And cummin with a rod.
>   Is bread-corn crushed ?
>   Nay ! he will not for ever be threshing it ;
>   But he rolleth his cart-wheel over it,
>   And separateth it without crushing it.
>   This also cometh forth from the Lord of hosts ;
>   Wonderful is His counsel, great is His wisdom ! "

Here three different methods of threshing are mentioned, all of which are still practised in Palestine at the present day—the beating out of seed with a stick; the dragging over the grain a heavy wooden sledge shod beneath with flint or iron; and the driving over it a cart with heavy wheels drawn by oxen, so that the grain is separated from the straw both by the action of the wheels and by the feet of the oxen.

These methods, Isaiah says, cannot be used indiscriminately upon all kinds of seed. Fitches and cummin—the two terms in the original denote different varieties of the same species of plant, the seed of which is used extensively in the East for flavouring purposes — would be destroyed by the rougher methods which are suitable for the cereal crops, wheat and barley. And even these latter crops are not treated in such a way as to crush and damage them. The cart-wheel is turned upon them just sufficiently to separate the grain from the chaff, but no more. All is done in due measure, as circumstances require.

Here *threshing*, like *ploughing*, typifies the divine discipline. There is, the prophet seems to imply, a different measure of discipline which is suited to different societies and to different individuals. The kind of discipline which might crush one man, or one class of men, is adapted—nay, is necessary—in all its rigour, to bring out the best good in another.

"This also cometh forth from the Lord of hosts;
Wonderful is His counsel, great is His wisdom!"

"To Isaiah there is something very impressive in the peasant's subtle yet unpretentious knowledge of his craft; he is like a part of nature, and his wisdom seems a direct emanation from the infinite Wisdom to which all things owe their being."[1] If this Wisdom —he would have us reason—carries on its face its own triumphant vindication in these simple operations of every-day life, can we not trust that it is acting so as to bring about the best results in the greater worldly vicissitudes which affect the fate of nations and individuals?

The application of Isaiah's parable to the circumstances of the present time is so obvious that it need not be laboured any farther. Yet there is, I think, one aspect of it which we need more especially to take to heart.

God is ploughing in order that He may sow. What is to be our own part in that seed-plot, both as a nation and as individuals? We are, perhaps, so much occupied in emphasizing the very true fact that we are fighting in the cause of righteousness and humanity, that we forget to ask ourselves whether we represent that cause as worthily as the occasion demands. God, we believe, has put His sword into our hands; but are we as fitted to wield it as we might be? If not, may it not be that the discipline which we are called upon to undergo—and it seems, according to all human probability, to be likely to

---

[1] Skinner, *Cambridge Bible, ad loc.*

prove long and severe—may be most necessary in order to bring out the higher possibilities of which we are capable ? There is in us, no doubt, much chaff which needs to be removed by threshing. I need not specify its character; we can, with a little thought, determine that for ourselves—the moral slackness which comes of too much luxury and pleasure-seeking, the physical inertia produced by prosperity and selfishness, all this and what not else besides ? it has, we may well believe, all got to be purged away, whether we like it or not.

Only let us strive to realize the true character and purpose of the divine discipline, and to bend ourselves with honest and true intention to hasten and to further its beneficial results; that so we may, each and all, so far as in us lies, add our handful to the harvest of good seed which we trust that the future is to produce.

X.

HABAKKUK AND THE CHALDÆANS.

"Behold, his soul is puffed up, it is not upright in him :
But the just shall live by his faithfulness."—HAB. ii. 4.

THE prophet Habakkuk was concerned with a problem which, in many respects, offers an analogy
to the circumstances of the present crisis. He lived,
as we gather from his prophecy, during the later
years of the Judæan monarchy, when the most striking phenomenon in the political situation of Western
Asia was the rapid rise to power of the kingdom of
the Chaldæans.

The success of this kingdom had been brought
about by the vigour and initiative of a ruler named
Nabopolassar. The mighty kingdom of Assyria,
which for many centuries had dominated the fortunes
of nearer Asia, had passed the zenith of its power and
entered on a period of decline, when the Chaldæan
Nabopolassar succeeded in shaking off its yoke and
in establishing an independent monarchy at Babylon.
This was in the year 625 B.C. Eighteen years later
—in 607 B.C.—he called in the aid of barbarian hordes
from the north, and captured and destroyed the city

of Nineveh, the centre of Assyrian power. Thenceforward Assyria appears no more on the pages of history.

There was only one other great power in that part of the world with which Babylon had still to reckon. This was Egypt, who, profiting for the time by the downfall of Assyria, succeeded in obtaining a temporary footing in Palestine and northern Syria. In the year 604 B.C., however, Nabopolassar's son, Nebuchadnezzar, met Pharaoh Necho at Carchemish on the upper Euphrates, and inflicted a crushing defeat upon him. This was the death-blow to Egyptian pretensions to an Asiatic kingdom. Thenceforward it was bound to be merely a matter of time before the whole of Western Asia, including, among other small kingdoms, the kingdom of Judah, passed completely under the dominance of the Chaldæans. We read in 2 Kings xxiv. 7 that "the king of Egypt came not again any more out of his land: for the king of Babylon had taken, from the brook of Egypt unto the river Euphrates, all that pertained to the king of Egypt."

We must picture Habakkuk as prophesying at some date not far removed from 600 B.C., during the reign of the weak and wicked King Jehoiakim, who, having first assured the crown as the nominee of Pharaoh Necho, king of Egypt, passed, with the defeat of Egypt in Syria, under the vassalage of Nebuchadnezzar — against whom he subsequently rebelled, thereby entailing a legacy of misfortune upon his kingdom. We are told in 2 Kings xxiv. 2 that

" the Lord sent against him bands of the Chaldæans,
and bands of the Syrians, and bands of the Moabites,
and bands of the children of Ammon, and sent them
against Judah to destroy it, according to the word of
the Lord, which he spake by the hand of His servants
the prophets."

The moral problem which vexes Habukkuk's mind
may be briefly stated as follows.[1] Witnessing, as he
had done, the rapid advance of the Chaldæan power
and the downfall of nations before it, he can understand that God may be using this nation as His
instrument of justice, visiting upon the surrounding
nations, and not least upon the guilty kingdom of
Judah, their transgressions of the moral law and their
lapses from the divine standard of righteousness. But
why should the righteous God employ as His agent—
nay, why should He tolerate the existence of—a nation

---

[1] As ch. i. now stands, the connexion of thought is extremely
difficult. In vv. 2–4 the prophet's moral problem is the unchecked
existence of violence and irreligion within the kingdom of Judah.
Jehovah answers in vv. 5, 6*a* that this is to be punished by the raising
up of the Chaldæans, the description of whom immediately follows in
vv. 6*b*–11. This, however, raises *a second moral problem*, namely, why
so cruel and ruthless a nation should be permitted to devastate surrounding countries without divine interference (vv. 12 ff.). Clearly,
as the text stands, the prophecy cannot be all of one piece, for in
vv. 5, 6*a* the rise of the Chaldæans is pictured as *about to take place*,
whereas the whole point of vv. 12 ff. is the moral difficulty involved
in the fact that *their aggressions have been divinely permitted to go on
so long*. The simplest solution is that vv. 5, 6*a* are due to later
modification and interpolation, and that, as the chapter originally ran,
the problem is one only, namely, the divine toleration of the ruthless
violence of the Chaldæan. On this view the "violence" of ver. 2
is the same as that of ver. 9, namely, that of the Chaldæan invader.
This is the view which is adopted in the sermon.

which itself so flagrantly transgresses the divine law; which is so utterly ruthless, so callous and cruel towards the nations which it subdues, acknowledging no law but the law that might is right?

"How long, O Lord—he exclaims—
　How long, O Lord, shall I cry, and Thou wilt not hear?
　I cry out unto Thee of violence, and Thou wilt not save.
　Wherefore dost Thou shew me iniquity,
　And cause me to look upon mischief?
　For spoliation and violence are before me,
　Strife and contention rear their heads.
　Therefore religion is benumbed,
　And right will never go forth;
　For wickedness encompasseth the righteous,
　Therefore right goeth forth perverted" (ch. i. 2–4).

That is to say—this apparently triumphant exposition of the theory that fraud and violence are after all the ultimate factors, which carry the day in the world's politics, has a benumbing influence upon true religion within the prophet's own nation—the kingdom of Judah. The word which I have rendered "religion" properly denotes *divine instruction, divine guidance* as conveyed to the nation by the mouth of Jehovah's servants the prophets. We must recollect that the Hebrew prophets were politicians as well as teachers of righteousness—rather, it would be more correct to say, they were politicians *because* they were teachers of righteousness: as occasion arose, both within the nation itself and in the wider sphere of external politics, they pressed home upon the king and councillors of Judah a course of action of which the guiding principle was reliance upon

Jehovah and the strict performance of the demands of His moral law. This teaching, says Habakkuk, embodying the divine message, the divine code of action, *is benumbed, i.e.* it has lost its operative force, owing to the fact that it seems to be so flagrantly belied by the events which are going on in the world —the triumphant progress of the treachery and violence of the Chaldæans. Hence it comes about that " wickedness encompasseth the righteous "—and under the term " wickedness " the prophet seems to include the opposing policy of the godless and time-serving advisers of the nation—" therefore right goeth forth perverted," *i.e.* the course of action which is ultimately adopted by the nation of Judah as its guiding policy is radically unsound.

Then the prophet, with a few vivid strokes, draws a picture of the Chaldæan foe. He characterizes him as

> " That fierce and impetuous nation,
>   That stalketh through the breadth of the earth,
>   To possess dwelling-places not his own.
>   Fearful and terrible is he,
>   From himself doth his right proceed.
>   Swifter than leopards are his horses,
>   Keener than wolves of the evening;
>   And his horsemen come from afar,
>   They fly like a vulture hasting to devour.
>   He is wholly bent on violence,
>   And he gathereth captives like the sand,
>   And he—at kings he scoffeth,
>   And princes are his derision.
>   Yea, every fortress he derideth,
>   For he casteth up an earthwork, and taketh it "
>   (ch. i. 6-10),

And then Habakkuk, boldly yet reverently, puts
into plain words his indictment of God's government
of the world, as it seems to be manifested in the
circumstances of his day.

"Art Thou not from everlasting, O Lord?
My God, my Holy One, Thou dost not die.
O Lord, for judgment hast Thou ordained him,
And Thou, O Rock, for correction hath established him.
Too pure of eyes art Thou to behold evil,
And look on mischief Thou canst not;
Wherefore dost Thou look on treacherous men,
Wherefore art Thou silent when the wicked swalloweth up
        him that is more righteous than he?
And so he maketh mankind like the fishes of the sea,
Like the creeping things that have no ruler;
All of them he draweth up with a fish-hook,
He catcheth them in his net,
And gathereth them in his trawl;
Therefore he rejoiceth and exulteth.
Therefore he sacrificeth to his net,
And burneth incense to his trawl,
For through them his portion is rich,
And his food is plenteous.
Shall he for ever thus draw his sword,
And continually slay the nations unsparingly?"[1]

---

[1] Ch. i. 12–17. In ver. 12 the Hebrew text as it stands reads, "We
shall not die"; but Jewish tradition states that this is a scribal altera-
tion of an original text, "Thou dost not (or shalt not) die," made from
motives of reverence, the statement that God does not die being so obvious as almost (from the later Jewish point of view), to savour of impiety.
The reading, "Thou dost not die," gives perfect parallelism with
"Art not Thou from everlasting," in the preceding line, and with the
context—God is eternal and all-holy; why then should He tolerate the
wickedness of the cruel oppressor? On the other hand, the reading,
"We shall not die," if original, can only be taken as offering a partial
solution of the prophet's difficulty—the Chaldæan may be suffered to
oppress and chastise, but shall not be allowed to exterminate us.
Such a solution, however, would come too early in the prophet's train
of thought. He does not gain enlightenment till ch. ii. 3, 4.

Here we have a vivid simile—the weaker nations swept like helpless fishes into the tyrant's net, and the deification of his own warlike might as the only power which the lawless conqueror feels called upon to acknowledge.

Having thus stated his moral difficulty, the prophet in imagination stations himself upon his watch-tower, looking out to see what answer God will be pleased to vouchsafe to him.

> "Upon my watch-tower will I take my stand,
> And station myself upon the rampart,
> And I will watch to see what He will speak with me,
> And what He will answer to my impeachment" (ch. ii. 1).

He is not kept long in suspense :

> "And the Lord answered me and said,
> Write down a vision, and engrave it clearly upon tablets,
> So that he may run that readeth it.
> For the vision is yet for an appointed time,
> And it panteth towards fulfilment, and shall not lie.
> If it tarry, wait for it ;
> For it shall surely come to pass, it shall not delay.
> *Behold, his soul is puffed up, it is not right within him* :
> *But the just shall live by his faithfulness*" (ch. ii. 2).

These last words—the words of our text—contain Jehovah's summary answer to Habakkuk's difficulty ; and it is these words that the prophet is commanded (and the command is probably to be taken literally) to engrave in writing upon a tablet in some public place in characters so bold and legible that, as it is vividly expressed, "he may run that readeth it," *i.e.* so clear that even any one who hurries by cannot fail to note what is written, and to gather its meaning. "The different characters of the Chaldæan and of the righteous carry in them their different destinies." [1] The overweening pride of the former will in the end result in his own destruction—so it is implied, in contrast to what follows, "but the just (or righteous man) shall live—*i.e.* shall ultimately survive—by his faithfulness."

On the meaning of this latter clause I will speak more particularly in a few moments. At present let us notice how the indictment which is brought against the Chaldæan is treated in greater detail in a "parable" or "taunting proverb" (as it is termed) which follows. This is divided into five *woes* pronounced against the aggressor, denouncing in succession his rapacity and violence, the suicidal policy by which he aims at establishing himself as the all-highest war-lord, the bloodshed and fraud by which the magnificence of his cities is maintained, the barbarous glee with which he reduces conquered nations to a condition of impotence, and, lastly, his absurd and irrational idolatry. At the close of the last indictment "the prophet passes by contrast from the dumb and helpless idol to the thought of the living God, enthroned on high, before whom the earth must stand in awe":

"But the Lord is in His holy temple ;
Be silent before Him, all the earth" (ch. ii. 20).

---

[1] Driver, *Introduction to the Literature of the Old Testament*, p. 377.

Let us now return to the latter half of our text, which we reserved for final consideration :

"The just shall live by his faithfulness."

What is the sense which the word here rendered "faithfulness" is intended to convey ?

The fact is probably familiar to you that these words of Habakkuk are quoted by St. Paul in the Epistles to the Romans and Galatians [1] in passages in which he is working out his great doctrine of justification by faith : "the just shall live by faith." It is not possible, however, to establish an exact equation between the Greek term for *faith* as employed in the New Testament, and the Hebrew term as employed in our passage and elsewhere in the Old Testament. The Greek term describes an *active* quality, the deliberate and reasoned act of the whole of man's nature—the intellect, affections, and will—reaching forth in trust and reliance upon God. The Hebrew term, on the other hand, denotes, at least primarily, a *passive* quality—a quality of man's nature which would be more accurately described by the terms *trustworthiness, faithfulness,* than by the terms *trust* or *faith.* It is actually employed or in a physical sense, of the *steadiness* of an object ; [2] and, as employed, in a moral sense, it primarily denotes *steadfastness* of character. But though we have this difference

---

[1] Rom. i. 17 ; Gal. iii. 11. So also by the writer of Heb. x. 38.

[2] Moses' "hands were *steadiness*" (*i.e.* "were steady") when supported by Aaron and Hur (Ex. xvii. 12).

9

between the Old Testament and New Testament terms, it is quite easy to justify St. Paul's use of the Old Testament term in the New Testament sense, because it is the passive quality of steadfastness or faithfulness which naturally produces the active quality of a living faith in God.[1]

There are two other passages in the Old Testament which seem to me most happily to exemplify Habakkuk's use of the term. The first of them is in Isaiah: "Thou wilt keep him in perfect peace whose mind is stayed on Thee; because he trusteth in Thee. Trust ye in the Lord for ever: for in the Lord Jehovah is an everlasting rock" (Isa. xxvi. 3). The second is in Ps. cxii., an ideal description of "the man that feareth the Lord":

> "He will not be afraid of any evil tidings,
> For his heart standeth fast, and believeth in the Lord;
> His heart is established, and will not shrink,
> Until he see his desire upon his enemies" (Ps. cxii. 7).

It is this quality of *steadfastness* which, the prophet maintains, will win through to the end. Nor was his divinely-inspired confidence belied by the fact that the kingdom of Judah went down before the

---

[1] It may be claimed, indeed, that Hebrew *'ĕmûnā*, "steadfastness," frequently (as in the present passage) denotes the condition of character *produced* by faith, *i.e.* by πίστις in the New Testament sense. This is evident from the fact that the regular Hebrew phrase denoting "believe in" is *he'ĕmîn bĕ*, literally, "show steadfastness in." Thus the statement that Hebrew has no term which can be regarded as the equivalent of πίστις, and that therefore St. Paul's use of Hab. ii. 4 cannot be justified, hardly represents the fact.

Chaldæans, and was forced to undergo the discipline of the Exile. When he speaks of the just man who shall live by his faithfulness or steadfastness, he is thinking, not of the corrupt and godless kingdom of Judah as a whole, but of the faithful nucleus within the nation, which, as we know, *did* ultimately survive the captivity, and emerged from it as a purified community—the Jewish Church into which our Lord was born, and which was thus destined to become the seed-plot of Christianity; whereas the kingdom of the Chaldæans was ultimately wiped out by the Medo-Persian Empire, and is now to us a name, and nothing more.

Kingdoms built up upon unjust force and fraud have never survived. That is a fact which is writ large across the pages of history. It is moral qualities which ultimately gain the victory, and remain at the permanent basis of civilization. And a nation, in so far as it knowingly and of set purpose guides its whole course of action along the lines of Christian morality, may confidently commit its future to Him who holds the fate of kingdoms in His hand.

> "The vision is yet for an appointed time,
> And it panteth toward fulfilment, and shall not lie.
> If it tarry, wait for it;
> For it shall surely come to pass, it shall not delay."

XI.

THE RESPONSIBILITY OF THE INDIVIDUAL.

"And the word of the Lord came unto me again, saying, What mean ye that ye use this proverb in the land of Israel, saying, The fathers have eaten sour grapes, and the children's teeth are set on edge? As I live, saith the Lord God, ye shall not have occasion any more to use this proverb in Israel. Behold, all souls are Mine; as the soul of the father, so also the soul of the son is Mine: the soul that sinneth, it shall die."— EZEK. xviii. 1–4.

"For I have no pleasure in the death of him that dieth, saith the Lord God: wherefore turn yourselves, and live."—Ver. 32.

THE prophet Ezekiel was a member of the first band of Judæan captives which, together with the king Jehoiachin, was deported to Babylonia by Nebuchadnezzar in the year 597 B.C., eleven years before the fall of Jerusalem and the end of the Judæan kingdom. From his home in exile at Tel-Abib on the river Chebar, a branch-stream of the Euphrates, he carried on his prophetic work among the Jewish exiles, with his eye turned always towards his native land, where affairs, under the vassal-king Zedekiah, Nebuchadnezzar's nominee, were going from bad to worse, and the near-impending destruction of the Judæan monarchy was, to the prophetic insight, already plainly foreshadowed. Meanwhile, at Jerusalem itself, the prophet Jeremiah was endeavouring, all in vain, to recall the morally-guilty city to a sense of its religious obligations: and thus the two prophets—the one in Babylonia, the other at Jerusalem —were contemporary teachers, and had to face, very largely, a common political outlook, and a common phase of thought in the nation with whose instruction they were divinely commissioned.

We are not surprised, therefore, to find that the popular proverb which I have taken as my text, "The fathers have eaten sour grapes, and the children's teeth are set on edge," is quoted by Jeremiah as well as by Ezekiel; and Jeremiah likewise makes the assertion that in the future Israel shall no more have occasion to use it. The passage in the Book of Jeremiah is ch. xxxi. 29, 30. Let us see very briefly what the standpoint is which the two prophets are assailing, and what the newly-realized truth which they are inculcating.

The earlier religion of Israel was not, strictly speaking, based upon the doctrine which we call *Monotheism*, *i.e.* belief in the *existence* of one God only. The First Commandment, "Thou shalt have none other God but Me," enjoins indeed an exclusive allegiance to the one God Jehovah; but this religious injunction does not of itself involve the theory that Jehovah was the only God who had any real existence. There is, in fact, an abundance of evidence in the

Old Testament which proves that a different theory was current, even among the more instructed minds in Israel. Jehovah had made choice of Israel as a nation; and His relation to His people is commonly depicted under the figure of a covenant. He was, by the terms of this covenant, their *national* God, and the worship of any other god beside Him involved infringement of the covenant-relation; but this did not run contrary to the belief that other nations might in like manner have *their own* national gods, to whom they stood in a relation similar to that in which Israel stood to Jehovah.

The existence of such a belief in Israel in early times would take too long to prove at length. It will suffice if I take two illustrations of it. When Jephthah the Judge is endeavouring to settle Israel's differences with Ammon [1] by diplomatic means, he sends an embassy to the King of Ammon proving from past history Israel's right to the strip of territory which the Ammonites desired to annex; and, at the close of his argument, he uses these words: " Wilt thou not possess that which Chemosh thy god giveth thee to possess? So whomsoever Jehovah our God hath dispossessed from before us, them will we possess" (Judg. xi. 24). Here we must infer that,

---

[1] As a matter of fact, the Jephthah-narrative is formed from two parallel sources, one of which makes Ammon the aggressor, while the other originally assigned this rôle to Moab. The passage in question belongs to the latter strand of narrative. Chemosh was the god of Moab, not the god of Ammon. Cf. the writer's commentary on *Judges*, p. 298 ff.

for Jephthah, Chemosh appeared to possess as real an existence as Jehovah; the difference being that Israel was bound to Jehovah by terms of allegiance, whereas in relation to Chemosh no such bonds existed. Again, when David as an outlaw gets Saul into his power and magnanimously spares his life, we hear him afterwards reasoning with the king against the un-merited persecution to which he has been exposed, and he speaks as follows: " If it be Jehovah that hath stirred thee up against me, let Him accept an offering: but if it be the children of men, cursed be they before Jehovah; for they have driven me out this day that I should not cleave unto the inheritance of Jehovah, saying, Go, serve other gods " (1 Sam. xxvi. 19). To David, then, expulsion from Jehovah's inheritance—His *land*—was *ipso facto* equivalent to a command to acknowledge the allegiance of some other deity. He could not, according to the current Israelite conception of that age, worship Jehovah outside Jehovah's land, but must necessarily come under the domination of the deity who happened to be supreme over the land in which he might seek refuge.

For Israel, in fact, as for other Semitic nations, the national God was in early times regarded as a kind of divine counterpart of the national king, one of His main functions being to lead His people in battle, just as the human king was accustomed to do. This is the root-conception which underlies the old title *Jehovah Sebaoth*, " the Lord of hosts," *i.e.* the leader of the armies of Israel. You will remember that, in early times, the Ark, which was the concrete representation of Jehovah's presence in the midst of His people, used to accompany the hosts of Israel into battle. The Book of Numbers preserves for us the statement that, when the host of Israel struck camp in the wilderness and the Ark began to move forward, Moses was accustomed to say :

> "Rise up, O Lord, and let Thine enemies be scattered ;
> And let them that hate Thee flee before Thee"
>
> > (Num. x. 35).

Here we have, no doubt, the ancient battle-cry with which Israel moved forward to attack their foes ; and it illustrates very clearly the primitive conception of Jehovah as the national Leader of His people. The conception can be paralleled precisely from the literature of kindred nations. Assyrian kings commonly ascribe their military successes to the might of Ashur their chief god ; and other gods are sometimes distinguished by titles which point to their prowess and assistance in warfare. Thus we find Shamash, the sun-god, called "the warrior"; and Nergal, who was the war-god *par excellence*, is often described as "he who goes before me" in battle.

In adducing such parallels, I do not, of course, imply that in early times there was little that distinguished the religious conceptions of Israel from those of surrounding nations. On the contrary, it is quite certain that, from the time of Moses if not earlier, the conception of the God of Israel was invested with ethical and moral qualities which were not similarly inherent in the conceptions which kindred Semitic nations formed as to *their* own deities. Had this not been so, we could not explain the unique development which Israel's religion was destined later on to attain, and which made it the fitting preparation for Christianity. Only, together with these relatively high ethical conceptions—the outcome of special revelation—which distinguished Israel's religion even in early times, there was a setting of ideas as to the Deity and His relation to His people which Israel shared with other races of the same Semitic group, and which depends upon the fact that all races of this group sprang from a common stock.

The fact, then, being clearly recognized that the earlier form of Israel's religion involved exclusive allegiance to one God only, but did not exclude the belief that other nations likewise possessed *their* own national gods, whose real existence was not questioned by Israel, it is usual to define the religion of Israel at this early period as *Monolatry*, a term which means *the worship of one God only*, and is used in distinction from *Monotheism*, *i.e.* belief in *the existence of one God only*, the God of the whole world—a form of belief into which, under the influence of the prophets, the religion of the Old Testament was divinely destined to develop.

Now the conception of Jehóvah as national God only, limited in scope as it was, had naturally its limitations in practical application. It is one of these limitations only which I intend to notice this morning. The whole of Israel's conception of religion at this period seems to have been almost exclusively *national.* There was hardly a thought, as it appears, of religion as a personal matter between the individual and his God. Jehovah's covenant, indeed, was conceived as contracted by Him with individuals in the person of Israel's ancestors, the patriarchs; but these patriarchal figures are essentially the ideal representatives of the nation, and the promises are to their seed conceived as a *people*—the people of Israel. Thus, while there is in early times a strong corporate conception of religion, there are hardly any traces of an individualistic conception.

In accordance with this standpoint, the whole conception of moral responsibility is corporate rather than individual. Achan, a single individual, commits a trespass against Jehovah through appropriating part of the spoil of Jericho which had been placed under a sacred ban and ought therefore to have been utterly destroyed; and the result is that disaster falls upon the whole of Israel. When, again, his guilt is discovered, it is not sufficient that he alone should suffer the penalty, but his sons and daughters have to be executed with him (Josh. vii.). Or, to take another example, when in the days of David a famine falls upon the land, and the cause is traced to the guilt of Saul in violating Israel's covenant with the Gibeonites, this guilt can be expiated only by the execution of seven of Saul's descendants (2 Sam. xxi.). Such incidents seem to have been strictly in accordance with the highest ideal of religion at the time, because Jehovah, though conceived as full of compassion and gracious, slow to anger and plenteous in mercy and truth, keeping mercy for thousands, forgiving iniquity, transgression, and sin (a high and beautiful conception), was yet believed to visit the sins of the fathers upon the children and upon the children's children, upon the third and upon the fourth generation (Ex. xxxiv. 6, 7).

It would take far too long now to trace, even in the barest outline, the causes which contributed to the breakdown of the old conception of Jehovah as Israel's national God merely, and the birth of the wider and grander belief that He was the God of the whole earth, and that the so-called gods of other nations had no real existence. Suffice it to say that the higher conception first comes into prominence in the prophecies of two of the earliest of the writing prophets, Amos and Isaiah, whose missions fall in the latter half of the 8th century B.C., and are thus coincident with the widespread activity in Western Asia of the mighty power of Assyria. Given the conception of Jehovah as national God merely, but one among many other such national deities, and the spectacle of nations and their gods falling powerless before the mighty advance of Assyria might well have led to the conclusion that Ashur, the chief god of Assyria, was after all the most powerful of gods, and that Jehovah no less than the gods of other nations must bow before his might. This, indeed, was the deduction which was drawn by the Assyrian himself. "Hath any of the gods of the nations ever delivered his land out of the hand of the King of Assyria? Where are the gods of Hamath and of Arpad? Where are the gods of Sepharvaim, of Hena and Ivvah? And where are the gods of the land of Samaria?[1] Have they delivered Samaria out of my hand? Who are they among all the gods of the countries, that have delivered their country out of my hand, that Jehovah should deliver Jerusalem out of my hand?" (2 Kings xviii. 33–35).

But, at the supreme crisis, it was given to Jehovah's prophet Isaiah to divine the truth. The Assyrian, though he knows it not, is merely an instrument of chastisement in the hands of Jehovah, the God of the whole earth; he can go just as far as Jehovah wills, and then his overweening pride and "the glory of his high looks" shall incur the punishment which is their due (Isa. x. 5 ff.). Thus, out of crisis and calamity, there emerged a great conception, a great belief, which was destined to be fruitful for all future ages—the conception of a supremely moral and righteous Deity

---

[1] This sentence, which does not occur in the Hebrew text from which our English versions are translated, is supplied from the Lucianic recension of the Septuagint, which reads καὶ ποῦ εἰσὶν οἱ θεοὶ τῆς χώρας Σαμαρείας; Its insertion is indispensable, the subject presupposed by "have they delivered?" etc., being clearly the gods of Samaria, and not the ods of other nations previously mentioned.

who directs, not merely Israel as a nation, but the course of affairs throughout the universe.

Coming down a century and more after the close of Isaiah's ministry, we reach the period of the fall of the kingdom of Judah, and the ministries of Jeremiah and Ezekiel. With the break-up of the national life, and amid the calamities which beset the kingdom, there arose the belief that the then generation was suffering, not for its own fault, but for the sins of its ancestors, and thus the proverb was coined, " The fathers have eaten sour grapes, and the children's teeth are set on edge." " Not so," say Jeremiah and Ezekiel, " but, rightly conceived, moral responsibility lies with the individual." Jeremiah's teaching in this connexion is bound up with his beautiful conception of the New Covenant, written no longer, like the Old Covenant, upon tables of stone, but upon the individual hearts of its recipients (Jer. xxxi. 26 ff.). Ezekiel's argument, as embodied in ch. xviii. from which I have taken my text, is well worthy of careful study; for there is scarcely any passage in the prophets which contains thoughts of more enduring value, or more nobly expressed. " Behold, all souls are Mine; as the soul of the father, so also the soul of the son is Mine: the soul that sinneth, it shall die. . . . For I have no pleasure in the death of him that dieth, saith the Lord God: wherefore turn yourselves, and live." Thus, with the growth of a full doctrine of monotheism, there emerged, as it was bound to do, the doctrine of the moral responsibility of the individual soul to its Maker and Sustainer.

I have chosen this subject to-day because it seems to stand in close connexion with my subject of last Sunday morning.[1] In speaking then of the proposed excision from use in public worship of the Imprecatory Psalms, and in deprecating, upon the whole, such a proceeding, I observed that there *are* certain such passages the use of which by Christians cannot be defended, because they are of a piece with the Old Testament conception, according to which the sins of the fathers are rightly visited on the children, seeking as they do to involve the relatively innocent in the punishment of the guilty. I instanced, you may remember, Ps. cxxxvii., where there occur the terrible words :

> " Blessed shall he be that taketh thy children,
>   And throweth them against the stones " ;

and Ps. cix., which contains a lengthy section breathing imprecations, not merely against the guilty wicked, but also against his wife and children and remoter descendants.[2] This is a standpoint which, as we have seen this morning, became obsolete in the Old Testament itself, in face of such higher and nobler teaching with regard to individual responsibility as Jeremiah and Ezekiel were divinely inspired to convey.

Here we have a thought which has a direct bearing upon events at the present time.

---

[1] See Sermon No. XVIII, p. 216.   [2] P. 230.

It has a bearing, in the first place, upon the clamour for reprisals which, in face of the recent air-raids, has been so insistent in certain sections of the Press. No truly Christian nation can adopt methods of warfare which are knowingly and deliberately aimed at involving non-combatants, relatively innocent women and children, in sudden and terrible death and mutilation by way of reprisal. "All war," we are told by some, "consists in reprisal"; but no one, I presume, is really deceived by such a statement into confusion of legitimate acts of war, such as the bombing of munition-works, railways, or aerodromes, with air-raids upon defenceless towns, made simply with the object of repaying frightfulness with frightfulness. We are fighting for a high ideal of humanity and civilization; and it would be preferable that the world should be wiped out in an instant by an act of God, rather than that we should forget our mission, and descend to the methods of our opponents.

And, secondly,—and this is a question which will have to be faced in the future,—we dare not, as Christians, identify the whole German nation with the ruling and directing powers, and declare that each and all belonging to that nation are equally guilty and unforgivable. This war, which is aimed at the liberation of the world from an intolerable menace, and which, if it is not carried through to completion, might as well not have been fought at all, has, as one of its aspects, the liberation of Germany itself in the truest sense, and the creation of a new and regenerate state in which, please God, such national elements as make for true culture and humane progress may be set in a right direction, and may be enabled to expand and develop themselves for the world's good.

It is not for us to include in one irredeemable whole deceivers and deceived, and to assert, out of our puny understanding, that there is no hope. As well might some arrogant judge of humanity have ventured to assert that the whole world was so sunk in wickedness that there was no hope of its regeneration at the time when our Lord was pleased to become incarnate on this earth.

Let us then, if we can at present find no just grounds for such a hope as I have ventured to indicate, at least be content to suspend our judgment, and to leave the matter in the hands of God, Who looks, as we have seen, upon individual responsibility, Who is too pure of eyes to confuse the innocent with the guilty, and Who, even to these latter, holds out the offer of amendment and restoration: "I have no pleasure in the death of him that dieth, saith the Lord God : wherefore turn yourselves, and live."

XII.

THE SERVANT OF JEHOVAH AND HIS MISSION.

" Yet it pleased the Lord to bruise him;
He hath put him to grief :
When his soul shall make an offering for sin,
He shall see his seed, he shall prolong his days,
And the pleasure of the Lord shall prosper in his hand.
He shall see of the travail of his soul and shall be satisfied :
By his knowledge shall my righteous Servant make many
    righteous ;
And their iniquities *he* shall bear.
Therefore will I divide him a portion with the great,
And he shall divide the spoil with the strong ;
Because he poured out his soul unto death,
And was numbered with transgressors :
Yet it was he that bare the sin of many,
And made intercession for the transgressors."—Isa. liii. 10–12.

THE call to a Mission of Repentance and Hope comes, I believe, to many minds with a certain amount of perplexity. We have been reminded, times without number, from the pulpit and in the Press, that this war is a war in which the issue between right and wrong is more clearly defined than perhaps ever before in the course of history. We feel, in our inmost consciences, that we as a nation are *in the right*; that we have taken up the sword to defend the cause of justice, the cause of the weak against the oppressor, the cause of civilization rightly so called—in short, *the cause of God.* We see, in this stupendous struggle, a reflection of that Apocalyptic struggle described in the Book of Revelation : " There was war in heaven : Michael and his angels fought against the dragon ; and the dragon fought and his angels " (Rev. xii. 7) ; and we believe from the heart that we are on the side of the Archangel Michael against the powers of darkness.

Why, then, it is asked, do we need a call to *repentance* ? All this suffering which has come upon us is the direct result of our having taken sides in defence of the right. Why should we be urged, as a nation, *to repent,* as though it were to be regarded as the divine *chastisement* for national *sin* ? Those who raise this objection have, as it seems to me, advanced a genuine problem : and it is to the solution of this problem offered by Old Testament prophecy that I propose to call your attention this morning.

Our subject is, the conception of the Suffering Servant of Jehovah as developed in that great section of the latter half of the Book of Isaiah which extends from ch. xl. to ch. lv. Here we have the idea of suffering undertaken vicariously for the redemption of the world. The conception of the Servant as an *ideal* personage comes out in four great passages which are poetical in form in the original Hebrew, and which very likely existed as separate pieces before the composition of the prophecy in which they are now embodied; though there can be no doubt that they were placed in their present position by the writer of chs. xl.–lv. as a whole, who uses them to work out the lesson which he has in view.

In speaking last month of the teaching of Hosea and Amos, I was dealing, as you may remember, with the two earliest of the writing prophets, whose career is to be placed at about the middle of the 8th century B.C. This morning, in speaking of Isa. chs. xl.–lv. we are making an advance of two centuries. Though these chapters are incorporated with the prophecies of Isaiah, who was a prophet of the kingdom of Judah in the latter half of the 8th century, a little subsequently to the time of Amos and Hosea, yet they make no claim to have been written by the 8th century prophet, and their contents prove them to be the work of a later prophet who wrote towards the close of the Babylonian captivity of Judah. The Babylonian Exile, so far from being predicted as something future, forms an understood element in the situation of the prophet and those for whom he is writing. On the other hand, deliverance from exile *is* predicted; and the opening verse of ch. xl. strikes a note of encouragement and consolation. Jerusalem has already received at Jehovah's hands double for all her sins, and deliverance and restoration are near at hand. Cyrus, who is to be Jehovah's instrument in bringing about this restoration, has already advanced upon his career of conquest; and the fact of his rise upon the horizon of the times is triumphantly cited as *the fulfilment of prophecy*, the fulfilment of an event which Jehovah has announced in time past by the mouth of His prophets, and so a proof of His almighty power as against the powerlessness of the heathen gods who are unable to point to any instance of an event predicted by them which has found fulfilment.   This fact, when taken by itself, is amply sufficient to prove that the prophecy cannot have been written by Isaiah in the 8th century B.C. ; since it may legitimately be asked what becomes of this argument for Jehovah's power to do yet greater things for His people, based upon the fact that He has already brought about past predictions through having raised up Cyrus to do His good pleasure, if the prophecy was spoken or written more than a hundred years before Cyrus was born ? The date of Isa. xl.–lv. is fixed, then, within fairly narrow limits.   The union of the Medes and Persians into one empire by Cyrus, the event which first brought him into prominence as a conqueror, took place in 549 B.C. ; the return of Israel from exile by edict of Cyrus is placed in 538 B.C.   The inference therefore is that some time during the eleven years which intervene between these two dates this prophecy of restoration was written down.   The distinct authorship of Isa. xl.–lv. having been established along the lines thus briefly indicated, it has become customary to speak of the unknown exilic author as Deutero-Isaiah.

Taking the evidence of the prophecy of chs. xl.–lv. as a whole, it is clear that the Servant of Jehovah is a collective personification applied to the nation of Israel.   There is, however, a certain amount of difficulty arising out of the contrast between the real and the ideal Israel; and this—if we are really to understand the prophecy—we must proceed to examine.   Let us notice, first, the four passages which I have already mentioned as specially marked by their poetical form, and as perhaps originally existing as separate pieces.   In all of these the Servant appears as an idealized personality, and we may describe them as *the Servant-poems.*

The first of them is found in ch. xlii. 1–4. Endued with the spirit of Jehovah, the Servant is represented as charged with a mission which is world-wide in scope: "He shall bring forth judgment to the nations ('judgment,' *i.e.* true religion regarded from its practical side as the regulating factor of human life). . . . He shall not fail nor be discouraged till he have set judgment in the earth, and the coast-lands (*i.e.* the lands beyond the western sea) shall wait for his in-struction."   So vast a movement is not to be accom-plished through violent means, or by a great upheaval. It is to be a beneficent work, characterized by gentle, steady progress.

"He shall not cry nor lift up,
Nor cause his voice to be heard in the street.
A bruised reed shall he not break,
And a dimly-burning wick shall he not quench;
He shall bring forth judgment in accordance with truth."

Ch. xlix. opens with the second great passage which describes the work of Jehovah's ideal Servant. Here the Servant himself is introduced as speaking, and announcing his mission to the world at large. He describes himself as Jehovah's efficient instrument:

> " He hath made my mouth like a sharp sword ;
> In the shadow of His hand hath He hid me ;
> And He hath made me a polished shaft ;
> In His quiver hath He kept me close :
> And He said to me, Thou art My Servant ;
> Israel in whom I will be glorified."

Here for the first time we have a proof that the *ideal* Servant is in some sense *Israel*, *i.e.* in some sense the nation or its representative. But that the term "Servant" is not here, as elsewhere in the prophecy generally, applied to the whole nation in actuality is clear from vv. 5 and 6, where the Servant represents himself as charged with a mission to his nation in the first place, and then to the Gentiles. The words of Jehovah, as addressed to him, are :

> "It is a light thing that thou shouldest be to Me a Servant,
> To raise up the tribes of Jacob,
> And to restore the preserved of Israel :
> I will also give thee for a light to the Gentiles,
> That My salvation may be unto the end of the earth."

In ch. l. 4–9 we meet with the third poem which concerns the ideal Servant. Here again it is the Servant who speaks, dwelling upon the theme of his mission, to which allusion was made in the earlier passages. Now, for the first time, it is made clear that the mission will involve much difficulty, much suffering, pain, and loss to Jehovah's agent. All this, however, he has well weighed beforehand; and he expresses his determination to go forward in the strength of the Lord Jehovah, whatever may betide him.

This indication of the suffering which is in store for Jehovah's Servant in the accomplishment of his mission prepares the way for the fourth and last great passage which deals with the ideal Servant (chs. lii. 13–liii. 12). Here the poem takes the form of a description of the Servant's sufferings, death, and resurrection, apparently put into the mouth of the "many nations" and "kings" mentioned in lii. 15, who express their wonder as the meaning of the spectacle of which they have been witnesses dawns upon them. It is this passage from which I have taken my text.

So much, then, as regards the four poems which speak of the ideal Servant. There are, however, other passages in the prophecy of chs. xl.–lv. in which the title "Servant of Jehovah" is applied to the nation of Israel as a whole; and in some of these his characteristics appear definitely to fall short of the ideal. Assuming that the ideal Servant of the poems is a collective personification, as elsewhere in Deutero-Isaiah's prophecy, let us see very briefly whether it is not possible—in spite of the contrast between the ideal and the real—to trace a consistent presentation of the office and work of the Servant throughout chs. xl.–lv. as a whole.

The language used of Israel in the first passage (ch. xli. 8 ff.) in which the nation is spoken of under the title of "Servant of Jehovah" implies very strongly the sense of *vocation*. The Servant has been "chosen," "taken hold of from the ends of the earth, and called from the corners thereof." The vocation means that Israel has been selected as the recipient of a special revelation, and is called to extend this revelation to the world at large. This is the meaning of the presentation of the nation through the Exile; this is to be the purpose of the restoration which is so soon to take effect. We have this idea worked out in ch. xlii. 6, a striking passage in which the Servant is described as appointed as a "covenant-people," "a light to the nations." In ch. xlii. 19, we find an expression used to describe the Servant which is rendered in the R.V., "he that is at peace with Me," with two marginal alternatives, "made perfect," or "recompensed." Here the Hebrew expression is *m^eshullām*, a word which is the equivalent of the Arabic *muslim*, "the surrendered one," or follower of *Islâm*, *i.e.* the religion of "surrender." It is preferable, therefore, to assume that the Hebrew term also means "the surrendered one"; *i.e.* the Servant is, or should be, *surrendered to Jehovah*, the facile instrument of His will for the effecting of His purposes in the world.

Such is the ideal for the nation as a whole; but how different is the real! The Servant is blind and deaf to his vocation. Seeing many things, he observes

not; his ears are open, but he hears not. Thus, when
next we find the *ideal* Servant mentioned, *i.e.* in ch.
xlix. 1–6, where he is represented as speaking, it is
clear that the conception has been narrowed down.
The Servant is still Israel; for in ver. 3 we read the
statement, " He said unto me, Thou art My Servant;
Israel in whom I will be glorified." And yet not
Israel as a whole, for ver. 6 describes part of his
mission (*i.e.* the preliminary part) as being " to raise
up the tribes of Jacob, and to restore the preserved of
Israel." Here, then, we are dealing with an Israel
within Israel, the faithful worshippers of Jehovah
upon whom the hope of the nation must be centred.

The narrowing of the conception in this passage
by no means implies, however, that the prophet has
abandoned his ideal in regard to Israel as a people.
Throughout the earlier section of his prophecy (*i.e.* down
to the end of ch. xlviii.) we may see him struggling
with the fact that this ideal is not at present realized
in the nation as a whole; but he is strong in his per-
suasion, or (it may fairly be said) *his conviction*, that
the ideal *can* and *will* be realized in the near future.
Ch. xliv. is very important in this connexion. We
notice that in vv. 1 and 2 the very same expression
(" He that formed thee from the womb ") is used of
Israel's vocation as is employed in xlix. 5 of the vocation of the ideal Servant. The chapter then goes on
to describe Israel's moral regeneration, when the nation
as a whole shall be dedicated to Jehovah. The
culmination of the chapter appears to be reached

in vv. 21 and 22, where, after reiteration of the Servant's predestination for his mission, there follow the gracious and tender words, " I have blotted out as a thick cloud thy transgressions, and as a cloud thy sins : return unto Me, for I have redeemed thee."

In the second half of the prophecy we read no more of the shortcomings of the actual servant Israel, the prophet appearing to become more and more absorbed in the mission of his idealized figure. Ch. xlix. 7 employs the same expression, "a covenant-people," as we have already noticed in xlii. 6 ; and here (in xlix. 7) it is brought into connexion with a description which speaks of the Servant as "him whom man despiseth, whom the people abhorreth, a servant of rulers"—a description which is doubtless intended to pave the way for the final scenes.

It ought not to pass unnoticed that there is apparently a point of connexion between the un-exampled sufferings of the Servant, with the expla-nation of them which is given in the final poem (liii. 5 ff.), and the opening of Deutero-Isaiah's pro-phecy, xl. 2, where it is stated that Jerusalem has received at Jehovah's hand *double* for all her sins.   It is a fact of history that Israel has sinned in the past and received punishment during the Exile ; but why has the penalty been so far in excess (double) of the crime ?   This is the problem of which we are to find the solution in the two last Servant-poems.

Let us briefly review these passages. Now at length it becomes quite clear that the mission en-

trusted to the Servant can be accomplished only
through much suffering. His contemporaries fail to
understand his steadfast purpose; he is greeted, not
with enthusiasm, but with scorn and loathing. None
like him has ever understood what sorrow means.
He experiences to the full the sharp pain of isolation,
the agony caused by the misinterpretation of the
active sympathy which he has to proffer. Yet in
spite of all he still persists. In the teeth of persecution he sets his face like a flint, for the Lord
Jehovah is his helper, and he knows that he shall not
be put to shame. Finally, in the pursuit of his aims,
he voluntarily suffers a cruel death, allowing himself
to be numbered with transgressors, and undergoing
the death and burial of the worst of felons.

But it is through death that the purpose of his
life is worked out. His death is a guilt-offering: his
sufferings are vicarious. Jehovah has been pleased to
smite him in order that his blood may become the
seed of a renewed community. Thus he is pictured
as rising again from the dead, and as gazing with
satisfaction upon the result of his labours, knowing
that, through his uttermost surrender, God's purpose
has been accomplished to the full.

As regards the speakers in ch. liii., we have
already noticed that they appear to be—not other
Israelites who are speaking about a select few (or a
single figure) within their own nation, but—the
heathen nations of the world who are speaking about
the nation of Israel, regarded here as a righteous unit.

That is to say, the prophet's conception is again fitted to embrace in the mission of the Servant the mission of the nation at large. It is not a question of the redemption of the nation of Israel by its righteous members, but of the redemption of the world at large by the nation of Israel.

Nor need we be surprised if the ideal Servant, who elsewhere, as we have seen, seems to represent a righteous nucleus within the nation of Israel, should here come once more to answer to Israel as a whole. The measure of the nation's religion is found in its faithful members, be they many or few ; they represent the nation charged with a mission to the world at large : and regarded thus, in relation to the other nations of the world, as the conservator of the true religion, Israel as a whole is the righteous nation, and may be ideally invested with the attributes of Jehovah's Servant.

We conclude, then, that the Servant of Jehovah, as he figures in ch. liii., represents primarily Israel as a nation, passing through the sufferings and vicissitudes of the Exile, and, as it were, emerging from the tomb as the restoration from captivity in order to become the instrument of the redemption of the world.

We know, in the light of history, how this conception was realized ; for it is a great and wonderful truth (in no way minimized or explained away— rather, we may say, heightened and emphasized—by scientific study of the Old Testament) that the pro-

phecy finds its ultimate fulfilment in the Incarnation
and Passion of our Lord. He it was who became in
His Incarnation the ideal Servant of Jehovah; and
the boldness of the lines in which the Servant is
depicted in Isa. liii. as an individual, makes the conclusion well-nigh irresistible that already to the prophet it was revealed in some mysterious way that his
conception was to find fulfilment in one great *Person*,
the Redeemer of the world.

Now very briefly, as regards the present situation.
May it not be that, just as the conception of the
suffering Servant, based in the first place upon the
mission and destiny of a nation, was gathered up and
fulfilled in the Person of our Lord Jesus Christ, so, in
and through vital union with Him, it may be again
realized in the destiny of a nation? Picture our
nation as charged by God with a mission to the world
at large—and we believe that this is so—may it not
be that this mission can only be accomplished through
suffering? We know it to be, as it were, a law of
our being that the attainment of high ideals involves
suffering. St. Paul is never tired of speaking of
Christians as sharing or fulfilling the sufferings of
Christ.

Looked at from this point of view, we may regard
our present suffering as a nation as in part *punitive*—
or as I should prefer to say, *chastening*—needful, *i.e.*
because in actuality we are unfit to realize our
vocation as Jehovah's Servant—blind and deaf to His

call; but also, thank God, as in large part *vicarious*, borne—and cheerfully, steadfastly borne—in realization of the fact that by and through it we are preparing ourselves for the carrying out of a great and world-wide mission, the realization of the most noble of ideals.

May God grant that this may be true of our nation, through our Lord Jesus Christ.

XIII.

ISRAEL'S MISSION TO HUMANITY.

"And the Lord said, Thou hast had pity on the gourd, for the which thou hast not laboured, neither madest it grow; which came up in a night, and perished in a night: and should not I have pity on Nineveh, that great city; wherein are more than six score thousand persons that cannot discern between their right hand and their left hand; and also much cattle?"

JONAH iv. 10, 11.

IN my sermon of a fortnight ago I dwelt upon the conception of the ideal Servant of Jehovah as drawn by the unnamed prophet of the Exile whose work is included in Isa. xl.–lv., and noticed the fact that the Servant typifies, in the first place, the nation of Israel, entrusted with a mission to humanity at large. As we observed, in the earlier half of his prophecy the writer is somewhat trammelled by the patent fact that Israel as a whole does not in actuality correspond to the ideal: the Servant is blind and deaf to his vocation—"Seeing many things, he observes not; his ears are open, but he hears not." This fact, then, leads the prophet to narrow down his conception of the *ideal* Servant, making it stand for an Israel within Israel who has a mission to his own nation

prior to (and yet only *preliminary to*) the wider
mission to the world at large. Finally, however,
strong in the sense of all that Jehovah holds in store
for His chosen people, the regenerative power of His
spirit, and the redemptive power of His grace, he
rises once again to the conception of the nation as a
whole fulfilling the function of the ideal Servant in
relation to the world at large, in face of suffering,
pain, and death.

We noticed that this wonderful conception was
destined to receive its adequate fulfilment only in the
Incarnation, Passion, and Resurrection of our Lord,
who was the ideal representative of the nation of
Israel; and then, bringing the prophetic ideal into
relation with the subject which is uppermost in our
minds to-day—the call to repentance and hope which
we take to be so intimately bound up with the crisis
through which we are passing—I ventured to express
the opinion that, just as the conception of the suffering Servant, based in the first place upon the mission
of a nation, was gathered up and fulfilled in the
Person of our Lord, so it may be the divine intention
that, in and through vital union with the Author of
our salvation, it should again be realized in the world-
destiny of this nation of ours, the truth that the
Christian Church (or some section of it from time to
time) may share or fulfil the sufferings of Christ being
guaranteed to us by the express teaching of St. Paul.

Adopting this hypothesis, we were able to discern
two explanations of the sufferings through which as

a nation we are at present passing. The first was that they may be to some extent *chastening* or *disciplinary*, in view of the fact that our nation as a whole is at present unfit to realize its ideal of vocation as Jehovah's Servant: the second was that they may, in part at least, be regarded as *vicarious*, *i.e.* as endured for the sake of humanity at large, it being a mysterious law of our existence that high results are most often (if not always) achieved only through suffering.

Since these two points are highly important in view of the moral difficulty which (as I noticed) has been raised in some minds as to why the present stress should involve a call to *repentance* when as a nation we have brought this stress upon ourselves through taking up arms in a cause which we believe to be *the cause of God*, I may be pardoned if I reiterate and enforce them. Picture our nation as Jehovah's Servant entrusted by Him with a world-mission (and of the fact of this vocation we have our guarantee in our national consciousness of the inherent rightness of our cause and its vital importance to humanity), yet we are bound to admit that as a nation we exhibit numberless faults and weaknesses which hinder our *ideal realization* of the possibilities of the call; and for these we need chastisement and repentance. Picture our nation once again as by the grace of God containing within itself the possibility of an approximation to the ideal of vocation; and we may from this point of view glory in our sufferings,

11

associating ourselves in all humility with Him " Who for the joy that was set before Him endured the Cross, despising the shame, and is set down at the right hand of the Majesty on high."

It is my purpose this morning to consider histori- cally (so far as may be done in a few minutes) the reasons why the exilic prophet's conception of Israel's world-mission failed of immediate realization in post- exilic times, or indeed of any realization however inadequate until, more than five hundred years later, it was taken up and fulfilled beyond all hope in the revelation of our Lord.   Let us notice very briefly the tendencies which were at work in a contrary direction ; and at the same time some of the passages which show that there existed, here and there, Jewish thinkers who were faithful to the wider ideal of the religion of Jehovah as destined to embrace within its sphere not merely the chosen people but the world at large.   Finally, we will centre our attention upon the most remarkable effort to keep alive in Israel the sense of a world-wide mission—the Book of Jonah from which I have taken my text.

One counter-tendency was undoubtedly the bitter resentment felt by the bulk of Israel for the oppression and cruel suffering which they had experienced at the hands of the heathen on the destruction of Jerusalem and during the Babylonian Exile.   Read the short prophecy of Obadiah, and you will find that it is a tirade of impending vengeance upon the neighbouring and nearly-related nation of Edom for the part which

this nation played against Jerusalem in the day of
her calamity. Recall, again, the terrible words of
Ps. cxxxvii. :

> "Remember, O Lord, against the children of Edom
>   The day of Jerusalem ; .
> How they said, Rase it, rase it
>   Even to the foundation thereof.
> O daughter of Babylon, that art to be destroyed,
> Happy shall he be that rewardeth thee.
>   As thou hast served us.
> Happy shall he be that taketh and dasheth
>   Thy little ones against the rock."

So long as such a spirit as this maintained a dominant
influence in the heart of Israel, it is obvious that it
must have proved an insuperable obstacle to any
thought of realization of the ideal Servant's mission
to the world at large.

A second counter-tendency was the hatred of
heathen idolatry. The religion of Israel had suffered
much in the past through the contamination of
outside influences—the nature-worship of Canaan,
the star-worship imported from the Semitic nations
lying to the east, Assyria and Babylon. In order to
safeguard the purity of religion in the future, after
the Exile, the possibility of such contamination must
be rigorously excluded. So thought some of the most
pious minds in Israel during the Exile and after. To
take the most outstanding and influential of such
thinkers. Ezekiel, who has been aptly described as
"the priest in the prophet's mantle," worked as a
prophet in Babylonia during the earlier part of the

Exile, being himself a member of the first band of
captives deported from Jerusalem in 597 B.C.   From
his home in exile he watches the last years of his
morally guilty but yet beloved city, and sees her as it
were rushing on her fate (which was to fall some ten
years later) in her neglect of Jehovah's ordinances
and addiction to the foreign cults of heathen deities.
Filled with confidence that there will still be a future
for his people and an eventual restoration from exile
he draws up a scheme for the religious worship of
the Zion of the future, the keynote of which is the
great conception of Israel as a holy people.   In order
that this may be carried out, Israel is to be hedged
round with ordinances for the maintenance of the
sanctity which Jehovah demands ; and this conception,
as it leaves Ezekiel's hand, allows no scope for the
admission of the heathen within the pale of Jehovah's
covenant : the idea of any participation by the nations
in Israel's blessings is foreign to the prophet's
thought.

This ideal, then, as formulated, ran directly counter
to the ideal embodied in the conception of the suffering Servant with his mission to humanity at large.
We cannot, of course, draw a sweeping distinction
and say that because the latter was right, therefore
the former was wrong.   The ideal of Israel as a holy
nation was a precious contribution to Old Testament
thought; though, as worked out in practice, a one-
sided ideal.   Had the nation of Israel, still imperfectly schooled in holiness, still blind and deaf to

the true significance of Jehovah's call, rushed into the wider field of the world in attempted realization of the ideal of Jehovah's Servant, the result could only have proved disastrous to itself, and of little benefit to humanity. The reason why modern missionary effort so often falls short of the fulness of its possibilities surely is that the lives of professing Christians, as viewed by the heathen, so often fail to offer any correspondence with the ideals of Christianity, as set forth by its preachers and teachers.

It was Ezekiel's school of thought which triumphed in post-exilic times. The idea of holiness, as reduced to practice, may be said to be mainly the contribution of priestly thought; and this explains the minute scrupulosity in matters of ceremonial which characterizes the religion of post-exilic Judaism.

There is, however, evidence that the wider and more noble ideal of the inclusion of the heathen within Jehovah's covenant was still kept alive in many minds. Let us notice some of the literature which embodies it.

The narrower school of thought found a vigorous and powerful exponent in the governor Nehemiah; and we read in his autobiography an account of the drastic measures which he took to do away with the marriages with foreigners which had been contracted by many of the Jews of Palestine in his times (Neh. xiii. 23 ff.; cf. Ezra ix., x.). It is highly probable that the Book of Ruth, though it evidently belongs in the main to the best period of

pre-exilic Hebrew literature and the narrative which
it contains bears the stamp of historical truth, yet
has been re-edited in post-exilic times, and given the
particular turn which it now possesses, as a veiled
protest against Nehemiah's measures in regard to these
foreign marriages. The writer draws attention to the
historical fact that King David himself derived his
descent from such a mixed union. The filial piety
of the Moabitess Ruth is finely illustrated. When
her son is born, she is compared to Rachel and
Leah " which two did build the house of Israel," and
she is declared to be better to Naomi her mother-in-
law " than seven sons." The case of Tamar, another
foreign woman who was an ancestress of David, is
also expressly cited.

We may notice, again, the astonishingly liberal-
minded sentiment expressed by the prophet Malachi
(who must have been nearly contemporary with Ezra
and Nehemiah), when—in contrast to the merely
formal and perfunctory performance of the requirements of religion against which he is protesting—he
boldly states that it is *intention* and *sincerity* which
really matter in religion, and that from this point of
view the heathen in their ignorance may be offering
worship more acceptable to God than the Jews themselves: " For from the rising of the sun unto the
going down of the same My name is great among the
Gentiles ; and in every place incense is offered unto My
name, and a pure offering : for My name is great among
the Gentiles, saith the Lord of hosts " (Mal. i. 11).

Then we have that wonderful chapter in the latter part of the Book of Isaiah, ch. lx., beginning, " Arise, shine ; for thy light is come." This prophecy probably dates from post-exilic times ; and in it Jerusalem is pictured as the religious centre of the universe, and it is promised that " nations shall come to thy light, and kings to the brightness of thy rising."

Nor must we omit to notice that beautiful little Psalm lxxxvii., where, after mention of Zion as loved of Jehovah, we read :

> "I will make mention of Rahab (i.e. Egypt) and Babylon
> Among them that know me ;
> Behold Philistia, and Tyre, with Ethiopia ;
> This one was born there.
> And concerning Zion it shall be said,[1]
> This one and that one was born in her ;
> And the Most High Himself shall establish her.
> The Lord shall count, when He writeth up the peoples,
> This one was born there."

Here we could scarcely have, expressed in few words, a more genial and comprehensive survey of the ideal possibilities of the scope of Israel's mission to humanity.

It is, however, in the Book of Jonah that we find the most remarkable protest against the narrow and self-centred attitude of post-exilic Judaism. This book has perhaps been more misunderstood than any other book in the Bible. It is ten thousand pities that a book which, when rightly interpreted, is found to embody the highest spiritual teaching, should,

---

[1] Or, if we follow the suggestion of the Greek version, which is probably more original, " Zion shall be called Mother."

through ignorance, have become the butt of scoffers, and too often—it may be feared—a trial to the earnest-minded in their endeavour to justify the experiences of the prophet at the bar of historical probability.

The fact is that the book is not historical, nor intended to be understood as history, but is from beginning to end *allegorical.* That the prophet Jonah, the son of Amittai, was an historical person appears indeed from the allusion in 2 Kings xiv. 25, where he is named as a pre-exilic prophet who announced to King Jeroboam II. his coming successes against the Syrian kingdom of Damascus. We may also assume that the fact of the prophet's preaching against the wickedness of the Assyrian capital Nineveh, may rest upon an historical tradition. But it is clear that the writer uses the facts as the basis of an *allegory,* framed to point the special truth which he desires to emphasize. The reason why this particular prophet was selected as the subject of the allegory probably was that, from the little that is known of him, he appears as *a prophet of vengeance,* hurling Jehovah's sentence of doom against Israel's hereditary foes.

If we turn to Jer. li. 34, we read the following plaint, in reference to the Jewish Exile: " Nebuchadnezzar the king of Babylon hath devoured us, he hath discomfited us, he hath made us an empty vessel, *he hath swallowed us up like a sea-monster,* he hath filled his belly with my delicates "; and a little later on (in ver. 44) there comes the following

promise of restoration from exile, given at the mouth
of Jehovah: "I will do judgment upon Bel in
Babylon, *and I will bring forth out of his mouth that
which he hath swallowed up.*" This simile, as used by
Jeremiah, may have been in the mind of the writer of
the Book of Jonah as he framed his story; at any
rate it furnishes a clue which aids us in arriving at
the inner meaning of the allegory.

Jonah represents *Israel as a nation*, charged with a
mission to *the heathen-world*, which is aptly symbolized
by the great world-power, Assyria. This mission he
deliberately evades by taking ship from Joppa to
Tarshish (*i.e.* Tartessus in Spain); thus making the
extreme West his destination, when he has been
appointed to the Far East. His plans, however, are
frustrated by Jehovah, who raises such a storm that
the ship is in danger of destruction. In the storm-
scene the piety of the heathen sailors and their
humanity seem intentionally to be brought into contrast with the apathy of Jehovah's prophet.

When Jonah has been cast into the sea, he is
swallowed up by a great fish specially prepared by
Jehovah; and, upon his liberation at Jehovah's command from the fish's belly, he receives a second
commission to go and preach to Nineveh. *Israel,
unmindful of his mission to the nations, is delivered
over to the power of Babylon* (the great sea-monster of
Jeremiah's simile); *and the release from exile is
accompanied by a second commission to act as Jehovah's
prophet to the world at large.*

This time the summons is obeyed; Jonah's preaching meets with unexampled success, and the whole population of Nineveh exhibiting practical proof of repentance, Jehovah's sentence is thereupon cancelled. But this issue is displeasing to Jonah. " I pray thee, O Lord," he says, " was not this my saying, when I was yet in my country ? Therefore I hasted to flee unto Tarshish : for I knew that Thou art a gracious God, and full of compassion, slow to anger, and plenteous in mercy, and repentest Thee of the evil." The prophet is willing to act as Jehovah's instrument in hurling His decree of vengeance against the sinful Ninevites; he will not be the witness of the divine mercy which spares and pardons. The writer leaves him, still morose and self-centred, apparently untouched by Jehovah's last appeal.

Here, then, we have a lesson for the future—and no doubt not a very acceptable one—which must be realized in thought and action if we are to rise to our national vocation as Jehovah's Servant. Surely it means that we are to be entrusted with a mission, not merely to friendly nations, but also to our erstwhile foes; and that, to accomplish this, we must, by God's grace, purge our hearts from the taint of hatred and animosity, be ready to forgive as we hope to be forgiven. Observe that it is not for me as a preacher to indicate *methods* (and at the present time such a course would be uncalled-for and unwise); I only have to speak upon *principles*. It was not (we may confidently assume) without good reason that the writer of the Book of Jonah selected as Israel's typical foe the city of Nineveh, the capital of the nation of Assyria which was in its day the scourge of Western Asia, maintaining its huge standing army by methods of frightfulness designed to strike terror into the hearts of weaker nations, and to wring from them the tribute, the payment of which left them impoverished and broken. And yet, according to our teacher, even Nineveh may repent and be forgiven by God, though God's prophet cannot bear the thought of it. "Should not I have pity on Nineveh, that great city; wherein are more than six score thousand persons that cannot discern between their right hand and their left; and also much cattle?"

May God help us! We have much to learn if we are to rise at all to the ideal of vocation as set forth in the mission of Jehovah's Servant. Of this, however, we may rest assured—that if the teaching of the Book of Jonah (and indeed the teaching of our Lord Himself) has any permanent value as a guide to action, unless we are prepared to exercise a forgiveness and a breadth of outlook which are, in quality, an approximation to the divine, we can never hope to attain to realization of the world-mission which God is now setting before us.

XIV.

THE SOUL ATHIRST FOR GOD.

"My soul is athirst for God, yea, even for the living God :
When shall I come to appear before the presence of God ?"
Ps. xlii. 2.

I STAND here this morning to address you for the
first time in virtue of the provision which connects a Professorship at the University of Oxford
with a Canonry in this Cathedral.

As Oriel Professor, it is to be my happy and
delightful task to spend my time in the minute and
detailed study of the Holy Scriptures, using, so far as
in me lies, the scientific methods of research, and
drawing upon the accumulated stores of knowledge,
which are the heritage of modern scholarship. Along
with this, it becomes my duty to spend three months
yearly in the service of this Cathedral, taking my
part in the worship which is offered here to Almighty
God, and endeavouring clearly to expound the abiding moral and spiritual value of these same Holy
Scriptures.

The close association of these two spheres of work
is, as it seems to me, peculiarly appropriate. It

brings most vividly before the mind a fact which is of
prime importance for Biblical study—the fact that,
while a right apprehension of the Holy Scriptures
depends upon a thorough and fearless use of all the
intellectual aids which God has placed within our
reach, this by itself is not enough to guide our steps,
and to lead us to our goal. We have to remember
that we are members of a Church which believes in
and proclaims the supernatural Presence of her Lord
in her midst, and the fact that He has promised to
give *Himself* to those who seek Him, in order that
He may guide them into *all Truth.* Thus we have,
in close association, the two great factors in Biblical
study, Intellectual Research, and Prayer ; the former
in itself (owing to the imperfection and limitation of
our human powers) of merely relative and partial
value, unless illuminated and set in the right direction
by the grace which God alone can grant in response
to the latter.

If there is one scene in Bible-history which a
student of the Old Testament might desire to appropriate as the type of his own experience, it is the
picture, so vividly drawn for us by St. Luke (St. Luke
xxiv. 13–35), of the walk to Emmaus, when the
two disciples—honest seekers after Truth, yet perplexed and disheartened at the failure of their own
theory of interpretation to explain the application
of the Scriptures to Him whom they rightly deemed
to be the Messiah—are approached and gradually
enlightened by their Risen Lord. "Beginning from

Moses and from all the prophets, He interpreted to them in all the Scriptures the things concerning Himself." How their hearts burn within them as they listen to His arguments, and realize their inspired truth! Little by little the scales fall from their eyes. Finally, He reveals Himself to them, fully and completely, at the breaking of the bread. May such a walk through life be the lot of all Bible-students; and then they may be quite sure that, whatever difficulties and perplexities may surround the interpretation of Biblical problems for the time being, God will gradually but surely enlighten their minds, and lead them at last to the full and perfect apprehension of the Truth.

It is my purpose, during these Sundays in August, to speak of different aspects in the relation of the human soul to God, as we find them illustrated in the Book of Psalms. This morning, as it seems to me, I could scarcely find a better introduction, both to the subject which I have chosen for this short course, and to my work as a preacher in this Cathedral, than the spiritual craving of the soul for God which must needs lie at the base of all true religion.

1. The Psalm from which I have taken my text forms, with the following Ps. xliii., one composition; and the present division into two separate Psalms appears to be merely accidental and erroneous. This is a fact which becomes clear if it be noticed

that the two Psalms taken together fall into three
strophes of nearly equal length, each rounded off with
the refrain :

> "Why art thou so heavy, O my soul ;
> And why art thou so disquieted within me ?
> O put thy trust in God ; for I will yet give Him thanks,
> Which is the help of my countenance and my God."

It is evident also from the rhythmical structure of
the two Psalms in the original, the whole composition,
with the exception of the thrice-repeated refrain,
being written in Hebrew elegiac rhythm, in which a
line of three beats is succeeded by a shorter line of
two beats.   This measure is, for the most part, lost
in the English versions ; but we may catch an echo
of it if we render, for example, a few lines of
Ps. xlii. thus :

> "Thirsteth my soul for God,
>   for the God of my life :
> When shall I come and behold
>   the face of God ?
> Tears have become my meat
>   by day and by night,
> Whilst they say unto me all the day,
>   Now where is thy God ?"

With this we may compare, from Ps. xliii. :

> "For Thou art the God of my stronghold ;
>   O why hast Thou spurned me ?
> Why must I go as a mourner,
>   oppressed by the foeman ?"

We are justified, therefore, in drawing upon both
Psalms when we examine the poem in order to
understand the situation of the author.

2. This situation it is not, I think, so very difficult to reconstruct.

The poet finds himself detained against his will in the neighbourhood of the Hermon range, near the sources of the Jordan, and far removed from the holy city Jerusalem. Very likely he may have been one of a band of captives halting for the night at the end of the third or fourth stage on the road from Jerusalem to Babylon. Such a halting-place would, at any rate, lie upon the course which would be followed along this journey; and we may perhaps therefore picture him as one of the captives deported to Babylon by Nebuchadnezzar after the capture and destruction of Jerusalem, and exposed, as appears from the Psalm, to the mocking taunts of his captors. That he was a Levite is extremely probable : for, as his thoughts dwell longingly upon the time that is past, or, to use his own expression, as he pours out his soul within him, he goes back to the days when he used to go with the throng, leading them solemnly to the House of God, with the voice of joyful shouting and thanksgiving, a multitude making pilgrimage. A prey to melancholy, he hears all around him the dull roar of the mountain-streams, as they come tumbling and dashing down the rocky gorges of Hermon ; and they seem to him to form the echo of his own unquiet thoughts :

" Deep calleth unto deep at the sound of thy waterfalls ;
All thy billows and thy waves have passed over me."

Yet, in spite of present circumstances, his trust in

God remains unshaken.   He can say, with firm
conviction :

> "By day will Jehovah command His kindness,
> And in the night His song shall be with me,
> Even a prayer unto the God of my life."

And so, as the long dark shadows creep down the
mountain-sides, and the shades of evening, falling on
the land, seem emblematical of the darkness enshroud-
ing his soul, his thoughts go out to Him with whom
there is no darkness, no perplexity, for whom the
night is as clear as the day, because darkness and
light to Him are both alike ; and he is able, with
fervent assurance of hope, to breathe the prayer :

> "O send forth Thy light and Thy truth ; let *them* lead me.
> Let them bring me unto Thy holy hill and to Thy
> dwelling-place ;
> That I may come in unto the altar of God,
> Even unto God, the gladness of my joy ;
> And upon the harp will I give thanks unto Thee,
> O God, my God.
> Why art thou cast down, O my soul ?
> And why art thou disquieted within me ?
> O put thy trust in God ; for I will yet give Him thanks,
> Which is the help of my countenance and my God."

3. It is upon the attitude of this Psalmist, and of
others like him, that I wish to dwell for a little while
this morning ;—the way in which the thought of God,
the sense of dependence on Him, seems to fill their
life, and to colour its whole background.   Like all
true poets, they are closely in touch with Nature, and
Nature always seems to speak to them of God.   The
everlasting hills of their native land remind them of

12

His strength and changelessness ; just as in its springs and streams they see reflected His life-giving power, without which man must faint and die.

> "O God, Thou art my God;
>   Early will I seek Thee.
>   My soul thirsteth for Thee, my flesh also longeth
>   after Thee,
>   In a barren and dry land where no water is"
>   (Ps. lxiii. 1).

We must notice also the great sense of *reality* which runs through their poems.   They are not the mere fanciful creations of idle minds, dwelling at ease. Many of them, on the contrary, are the outcome of intense personal stress and struggle.   They had their birth, it seems, in periods of suffering and persecution. Probably a great part of the Psalms included in the Psalter belongs to a period subsequent to Israel's golden age, dating from exilic and post-exilic times when the pomp and glory of the kingdom were things of the past, and oppression, hardship, and disappointment were commonly the lot of God's chosen people.   Many Psalms, indeed, may be as late as the period of persecution of which we read in the First Book of Maccabees, and may have been written by those witnesses to God whom the writer of the Epistle to the Hebrews seems to have in mind, when he tells us that "others had trial of mockings and scourgings, yea, moreover, of bonds and imprisonment: they were stoned, they were sawn asunder, they were tempted, they were slain with the sword:

they wandered about in sheep-skins, in goat-skins;
being destitute, afflicted, evil-entreated (of whom the
world was not worthy), wandering in deserts and
mountains and caves, and the holes of the earth "
(Heb. xi. 36–38).   And so, out of the hard and bitter
circumstances of their lives there sprang to birth these
poems of such wonderful truth and beauty that they
appeal to the hearts of men in all ages; just as the
anemones break into purple and red out of the rough
and stony soil of the hills of Palestine.

4. Now does not all this craving after God, this
spiritual thirst for Him and the finding in Him the
only true satisfaction, really witness to an instinct
which is innate in the human soul? We think at
once of the memorable words of St. Augustine,
"Thou hast made us for Thyself; and our soul knows
no repose, until it rests in Thee." These Psalmists of
whom we have been speaking, high as they seem to
rise upon the wings of faith, were after all men of like
passions to ourselves: their eye of faith was sometimes darkened, and doubtless they were not able
always to rise to the same height of hope and trust
and joy in communion with God. And it is to remind
us that this was so, perhaps, that we find included in
the Psalter a Psalm of such dreadful gloom and sad-
ness as Ps. lxxxviii., which begins:

"O Lord God of my salvation, I have cried day and night
before Thee";

in which all seems dark and not a ray of light pierces
through the clouds.

It was only our Blessed Lord Himself who, as perfect Man, His human nature unstained and unclouded by sin, constantly during His earthly life realized the highest possibility of communion of a human soul with God the Father. And because this was so, therefore all those passages of the Old Testament which express the hopes and aspirations of holy men after communion with God, and which put into words their sense of dependence upon God and their joy in His salvation, are all, as it were, gathered together by our Lord, and fulfilled in a way in which they never could be fulfilled by the Old Testament saints who first gave them expression. He too has willed, of His exceeding mercy, to take upon Himself all that makes for darkness, and failure, and the obscuring of the soul's right relationship to God, and to sum it up, in a way which we cannot fathom, in that loud cry which He uttered whilst He was breaking once and for all the powers of sin and guilt in those dark hours on the bitter Cross.

5. Is it not true that this same instinct of the soul to fly upwards towards God its Creator is inherent in ourselves to-day? "Thou hast made us for Thyself; and our soul knows no repose, until it rests in Thee." And may *we* not make our own the words in which these Old Testament poets express the spiritual craving of their souls—yes, and make them our own, perhaps, with an even deeper sense of conviction; since we know, in the life of our Lord, the height to which realization of communion with God

may rise ; and we know, too, the possibilities which lie open even to our weak and sinful humanity through union with the perfect life ?

The sense of this craving, the realization of this need, may lie buried and all but silenced, as it seems, in our hearts, as we move through life, for the most part, so far from God.   But it is *there*, hidden, though it may be, deep beneath the surface of our life.   And when, amidst the bustle and din of daily work and pleasure, we feel that this is not our rest, this is not our satisfaction ; when at times we have leisure for deeper thought, and, amidst so much that darkens and perplexes, we seem to ourselves to be no better than—

> "An infant crying in the night,
> An infant crying for the light,
> And with no language but a cry,"

it is that God, of His infinite mercy, is sending us times of recollection, drawing us back to Himself as the only source of spiritual satisfaction, the fount of those living waters which alone can quench the thirst of our souls.

There is a passage in one of Charles Kingsley's sermons [1] which seems to put into words the voiceless aspirations of our souls, as, in face of such a need, we seek to approach God through Christ our Saviour.   It is a sermon upon the Holy Communion ; and at its close, after speaking of " the intolerable burden of sin," he makes this prayer :

---

[1] *Town and Country Sermons*, No. xiv.

" Oh Lamb Eternal, beyond all place and time ! Oh Lamb slain eternally, before the foundation of the world ! Oh Lamb, which liest slain eternally in the midst of the throne of God ! Let the blood of life, which flows from Thee, procure me pardon for the past ; let the water of life, which flows from Thee, give me strength for the future. I come to cast away my own life, my life of self and selfishness, which is corrupt according to the deceitful lusts, that I may live it no more ; and to receive Thy life, which is created after the likeness of God, in righteousness and true holiness, that I may live it for ever and ever, and find it a well of life springing up in me to everlasting life. Eternal Goodness, make me good like Thee. Eternal Wisdom, make me wise like Thee. Eternal Justice, make me just like Thee. Eternal Love, make me loving like Thee. Then shall I hunger no more, and thirst no more ; for

> " ' Thou, O Christ, art all I want ;
>   More than all in Thee I find ;
>   Raise me, fallen ; cheer me, faint ;
>   Heal me, sick ; and lead me, blind.
>   Thou of life the fountain art ;
>   Freely let me take of Thee ;
>   Spring Thou up within my heart ;
>   Rise to all eternity.' "

" If thou knewest the gift of God,"—said our Saviour to the woman of Samaria,—" if thou knewest the gift of God, and who it is that saith unto thee, give Me to drink ; thou wouldst have asked of Him, and He would have given thee living water." And shall we

not hasten to reply with the woman, even though,
like her, we scarcely realize the full meaning of our
petition : " Lord, give me of this water, that I thirst
no more " ?

I can scarcely close without allusion to the bearing
of our Psalm upon the subject which is uppermost
in our minds to-day—the grave crisis at which we, as
a nation, are at present standing.[1]   For the Psalmist,
as for his nation (if we have interpreted aright the
situation of the Psalm), the future might, humanly
speaking, have seemed hopelessly dark, with no ray
of light to illumine its gloom.   Yet, as we have seen,
his trust in God, that instinctive feeling after the
divine guidance amidst the blackness of his earthly
night, fills him, in spite of everything, with sure and
steadfast hope for the future.

" O send out Thy light and Thy truth ; let *them* lead me."

May we make this our prayer, both for our nation
and for ourselves !   The measure of our Religion
is the extent to which we can, unreservedly, commit
our future to God, in sure trust that He is able
to bring light out of darkness, and to order all
things for the furtherance of His divine purposes.

May He grant us such a trust ; and lead us, by His
light and truth, so to adapt ourselves to His ends that
His will may be done on earth as it is in heaven.

---

[1] The sermon was preached two days before Great Britain's de-
claration of war with Germany on August 4, 1914.

XV.

COMMUNION WITH GOD.

"Into Thy hand I commend my spirit;
For Thou hast redeemed me, O Lord, Thou God of truth."
Ps. xxxi. 6.

IN pursuance of the subject which I have chosen for my morning sermons this month—aspects in the relation of the human soul to God, as illustrated by the Psalms—I deal to-day with *Communion with God*; the meaning which the consciousness of such communion possessed for the Psalmist whose words I have taken for my text, and the meaning which the consciousness of such communion may possess for us to-day in the light of the Incarnation of our Lord Jesus Christ.

1. The writer of Ps. xxxi. finds himself in a position of grave physical danger. He stands, as the champion of the worship of Jehovah, against those who give heed to *lying vanities*—all, that is, which is by nature opposed to the true Religion of Israel, whether it take the form of idol-worship, or the misleading oracles of false prophets, and the schemes of mere time-serving advisers of the nation.

So placed, he has become the object, not only of
scorn and dislike, but of active hatred.   His enemies
are planning to put him out of the way; and have
already made more than one attempt which has
only just failed to make him the victim of a violent
death.   Nor is this all.   Those whom he fancied that
he could count among his friends, who seemed in the
past to be to some extent in sympathy with his aims,
now treat him as one whose unpopularity may prove
contagious, and are at pains to disclaim and to avoid
all connexion with him.   Meeting him in the street
they hurriedly turn aside out of his path, or greet
him with a sightless stare as though · he were a
stranger.   In fact, so far as human sympathy and
assistance are concerned, he seems to stand in simple
isolation.   He can say of himself :

> " I am forgotten, as a dead man, out of mind ;
> I am become like a vessel left to perish."

But if his foes are rampant, and false friends have
cast him off, he knows that he is not forsaken by his
God.   Living as Jehovah's worshipper, and acting
always with an eye to His service, he has established
with God such a personal relationship as may well
avail him in the time of need—or, as he puts it, he
has made Jehovah his *Refuge*.   Thus he commends
his spirit—*i.e.* his life-breath which his enemies
would destroy—into the hand of God, feeling assured
that Jehovah, the God of truth—the faithful God—
will indeed deliver him ; and, strong in this confidence,

he can speak of deliverance as though it were already
an accomplished fact:

"Thou *hast redeemed* me, Jehovah, Thou God of truth."

For it is not without cause that he thus expresses
his assurance.   Already upon former occasions Jehovah
has *known* his soul in adversities, *i.e.* has taken notice
of him, and proved His concern for his welfare by
ready help in the hour of danger.[1]   His *times, i.e.* the
great crises of his life, at one of which he feels himself
now to stand, are in the hand of God, entirely at His
divine disposal; and *He* is able to deliver him out of the
hand of his enemies and pursuers.   Once and again his
human weakness may lead him to despond, and he may
seem to lose the sense of this divine companionship:

"And I—I said in mine alarm,
I am cut away from before Thine eyes":

yet, in spite of all, Jehovah has not forsaken him:

"Surely Thou heardest the voice of my beseeching,
When I cried for help unto Thee."

And thus, in strong assurance for the future, he is
able from the heart to exhort others who may find
themselves in like case to cleave unto his God and to
abide by hope:

" O love Jehovah, all ye His devout ones :
Jehovah keepeth faithfulness,
And abundantly recompenseth him that dealeth haughtily.
Be courageous, and let your heart gather strength,
All ye that wait for Jehovah."

---

[1] Cf., for this use of "know," Gen. xviii. 19 (in R. V.) ; Ex. ii. 25
(rendered, "took knowledge *of them* ") ; Am. iii. 2 ; Ps. i. 6.

If we inquire who was the author of our Psalm, we may notice certain indications which seem to lead us to a very plausible conclusion. Not only the position of affairs pictured by the poet, but also a number of expressions which are employed by him, may justify us in assigning the Psalm either to the prophet Jeremiah himself, or to one of his immediate disciples. This may be seen if we compare ver. 15 :

> "For I have heard the blasphemy of the multitude ;
> And fear is on every side,"

with Jer. xx. 10, "I have heard the blasphemy of many, and fear is on every side." The expression "fear is on every side," a very striking one in the original Hebrew, occurs six times in Jeremiah, and nowhere else but in this Psalm. Or again, ver. 19 :

> "Let me not be confounded, O Lord, for I have
>   called upon Thee ;
> Let the ungodly be put to confusion,
> And be put to silence in the grave,"

may be compared with Jer. xvii. 18, "Let them be confounded that persecute me, but let not me be confounded : let them be dismayed, but let not me be dismayed."

As regards the situation of the Psalmist—there were, we know, a number of occasions upon which Jeremiah stood in such imminent danger of death as is pictured in the Psalm. We may think, perhaps, particularly of the time when Jerusalem was besieged

by the Chaldæans, and the prophet was accused of
treason by certain courtiers who sought to put him
to death, as related in Jer. xxxviii. You may remember how they succeeded in casting him into a
damp and foul dungeon, from which he was rescued
by Ebed-melekh the Ethiopian. This may explain
the allusion in ver. 23 of our Psalm :

> "Thanks be to the Lord,
>   For He hath showed me marvellous great kindness
>   in a strong city " ;

or, more correctly, " in a besieged city."

2. We must pass on now to speak of that which
should make the words of our text of more peculiar
interest to us—the fact that they were used by our
Blessed Lord Himself as His dying words upon the
Cross : " And when Jesus had cried with a loud
voice, He said, Father, into Thy hands I commend My
spirit : and having said thus, He gave up the ghost."
Consideration of this subject should be of value as
aiding us to understand how our Saviour gathered up
into Himself and fulfilled the prophecies of the Old
Testament ; and also, as causing us to reflect, if only
brokenly and feebly, upon something of the meaning
of His Cross and Passion.

First of all, we ought to notice that our text, as
spoken by the Psalmist, is one of a great series of Old
Testament passages in which a good man expresses
his consciousness of the high and close relationship in
which he stands to God. They are very numerous,

especially in the Psalms, and many such will occur at once to your minds :

"Yea, though I walk through the valley of the shadow of
    death,
  I will fear no evil ;
For Thou art with me ;
  Thy rod and Thy staff comfort me" (Ps. xxiii. 4).

"I have set God always before me ;
  For He is on my right hand, therefore I shall not fall"
                          (Ps. xvi. 9).

"Lead me forth in Thy truth and learn me ;
  For Thou art the God of my salvation ;
  In Thee hath been my hope all the day long" (Ps. xxv. 4).

"The Lord is my light and my salvation ; whom then shall
    I fear ?
The Lord is the strength of my life ;
  Of whom then shall I be afraid ?" (Ps. xxvii. 1).

"Nevertheless, I am always with thee ;
  For Thou hast holden me by my right hand.
Thou shalt guide me with Thy counsel,
And after that receive me into glory.
Whom have I in heaven but Thee ?
And there is none upon earth that I desire in comparison
    of Thee.
My flesh and my heart faileth,
But God is the strength of my heart and my portion for
    ever" (Ps. lxxiii. 22–25).

But alongside of passages of this nature—and this is important to notice—we find another class of passages of quite a different character :

"O my God, I cry in the daytime, but Thou hearest not ;
And in the night season also I take no rest" (Ps. xx 2).

"Thou didst turn Thy face from me,
And I was troubled" (Ps. xxx. 7).

> "I will say unto the God of my strength, why hast Thou
>   forgotten me ?
> Why go I thus heavily, while the enemy oppresseth me ?"
>   (Ps. xlii. 11).

> "I am cut off among the dead,
> Like unto them that are wounded and lie in the grave,
> Who are out of remembrance,
> And are cut away from Thy hand" (Ps. lxxxviii. 4).

And as in the Psalms, so especially in the prophet Jeremiah do we seem to discern this double mood —at one time, apparently, perfect joy and communion with God; at another, utter despondency, and the very blackness of loneliness and desolation. At one time, "Thy words were found, and I did eat them; and Thy words were unto me a joy and the rejoicing of my heart; for I am called by Thy name, O Lord God of hosts" (Jer. xv. 16). But then again, "O Lord, Thou hast deceived me and I was deceived: Thou art stronger than I, and had prevailed: I am become a laughing-stock all the day; every one mocketh me" (Jer. xx. 7). In one mood, "Sing unto the Lord, praise ye the Lord, for He hath delivered the soul of the needy from the hands of evil-doers" (Jer. xx. 13). But then immediately, with scarcely a pause, "Cursed be the day wherein I was born" (Jer. xx. 14).

Now what is the reason for the existence of these two states of mind side by side; a condition of things in which, if we may say so, the faith and confidence of the one mood seems to a great extent to be dis-

counted and blurred and spoiled by the failure and
hopelessness of the other?

I know a rare old illustrated edition of Young's
Night Thoughts; and in one of the pictures the soul
is represented under the figure of a man springing
into the air towards the sky, but confined to the earth
by a chain fastened to his foot, which draws him back
when he would rise the highest.   The best of us, with
all his lofty aspirations and yearnings after God,
is as that man; and sin, and all the weakness and
ineffectualness introduced by sin, is that chain which
draws him back to earth, and spoils his best en-
deavours, and thwarts and hinders his longed-for
communion with his Creator.   And so it was that all
those Old Testament passages which speak in glowing
terms of communion with God and happy confidence
in Him could never be realized in anything like their
full meaning by the prophets and psalmists who gave
them utterance; but partook rather of the nature of
an *ideal*, an aspiration which remained as yet unful-
filled, and which, had it always so remained, might
have formed but the monument of failure and the
ruin of a spoiled humanity.

3. But we look at the human life of our Lord
Jesus Christ, and we see something so different from
the lives of these Old Testament saints, although
indeed so like to them.   We see a life thoroughly
human, yet at the same time thoroughly perfect and
without sin; a life in which the conscious personal
relationship towards God the Father is present from

the very beginning, and is maintained all through unbroken up till the hour of the Cross. And this is so not only because this Ideal Man is also very God— the Son of God, and because God's Son must always be present in closest communion with God the Father. This personal relationship towards God is seen existing also in Jesus *in that He is Man*—a true human being. And here let it be emphasized that we are speaking not of the union of His Manhood with His Godhead—the union of the two Natures in the one Person, but of the communion which He maintained *as Man* with God *the Father*, the consciousness that He was living on earth as in God's Presence, acting always with regard to this relationship to Him, doing His will with a cheerful, ready, unquestioning obedience.

And again, let us not imagine that because the Man Jesus was also Son of God, therefore this human relationship of communion with God and obedience to Him was rendered quite easy to maintain, and needed no kind of *effort* for its cultivation and realization. It is true indeed that it was made possible by the divine Sonship; but not on this account was the Man exempted from the need of constant conscious endeavour to maintain and to cultivate this condition of living and acting in the sight of God. Had He been so exempted, what need would He have had to rise a great while before dawn in order that He might pray to God, or to spend whole nights wrestling in prayer? What meaning, again, could we attach to that solemn and mysterious hour of agony in Gethsemane, that struggle of His human soul which the writer of the Epistle to the Hebrews so vividly describes: "Who in the days of His flesh, having offered up prayers and supplications with strong crying and tears unto Him that was able to save Him from death, and having been heard for His godly fear, though He was a Son, yet learned obedience by the things which He suffered"? (Heb. v. 7, 8).

Yes; in Jesus the Man there was the constant realization of communion with God, the constant bending of the will to God's will: and, because this was so, and no breath or taint of sin was suffered to come in even for one instant and obscure this relationship, therefore was our Ideal Man able to gather up into Himself all those Old Testament aspirations which speak of trust and confidence in God and intimate communion with Him—to sum them all up in Himself, and to fulfil their meaning to the uttermost.

"Thou art He that took Me out of My mother's womb:
    Thou wast My hope when I hanged yet upon My mother's
        breasts.
    I have been left unto Thee ever since I was born;
    Thou art My God even from My mother's womb"
                                        (Ps. xxii. 9, 10).
"Burnt-offerings, and sacrifices for sin, hast Thou not
        required;
    Then said I, Lo, I come;
    In the roll of the book it is written of Me:
    I delight to do Thy will, O My God;
    Yea, Thy law is within My heart" (Ps. xl. 9, 10).

And this was His offering, the offering of a perfect human will conformed in all respects to God's will,

13

uncrossed by diverse aims, unstained by sin, the sum and end of God's creation.

Just now we noticed that this conscious personal communion of Jesus, the Ideal Man, with God the Father, was maintained all through His life unbroken up till the hour of the Cross. And we have seen that this was the reason why He was able to make to God a perfect offering—led to the sacrifice like a lamb without blemish and without spot—His pure and perfect life taking the place of the imperfect ruined life of the race of men. But we come to the hour of the Cross, and we find there something dark and mysterious, which we cannot fully understand. We find Him, the sinless One, whose life had always realized the fulness of communion with God, entering now upon a new and strange experience. Was there anything in those Psalms of which we spoke which seemed to make for loneliness and weakness, distress, despondency, and failure? Now it is all laid upon the soul of Jesus. He who, throughout His lifetime, has realized the full ideal of unbroken communion of a human soul with God, now cries, in agony of spirit, "My God, My God, why hast Thou forsaken Me?"

We cannot thrust ourselves into that strange and awful mystery of suffering. We may picture the physical throes of pain upon the Cross, may mark those dark pools of blood which stain the soil of Calvary; but into that soul's agony we may not enter even in thought: we stand aside and veil our eyes in presence of a mystery too deep to fathom.

Only we know that into that bitter cry of abandonment was concentrated all that makes for human loss and failure; that there, in very deed, He bare our sins in His own body on the tree; that there He was made sin for us, who knew no sin, that we might be made the righteousness of God in Him.

4. But now all is accomplished: the pure Sacrifice has been laid upon the Altar; sin has been expiated to the full, and is taken out of the way; the darkness which shrouded the face of nature—fit emblem of that cloud which darkened the Redeemer's soul—has been rolled away. "It is finished," the Saviour cries, and once more He enters as Man into His own relationship of communion with God. He only has now to yield up His life; and calmly and of set purpose He chooses the words of our Psalm, "Father, into Thy hands I commend My spirit," and, having thus spoken, He breathes His last.

He gives, you see, a new and deeper meaning to the Psalmist's words. While this other was thinking mainly, if not solely, of the preservation of his life *from* death, trusting himself to God in order that God might deliver him from his human foes, our Saviour resigns His soul *in* death into God's hand, because He has Himself conquered the utmost powers of evil, and realized that ideal of communion with God which passes through death into eternity.

Nor does He need to add, with the Psalmist:

"Thou hast redeemed Me, O Lord, Thou God of truth";

for He Himself has worked out the Redemption of the world, and He Himself is God, the God of truth, the faithful God who has fulfilled the plan which He conceived from the foundation of the world.

But He hands on the words to us in all the developed fulness of their meaning. It is a Redemption from sin—from the power of sin—for all who are made one with Him, washed in His precious, cleansing blood, and sharers of His life—hidden with Christ in God. This it is that can enable us to commit our souls to God amidst every vicissitude, in life and in death, in sure trust in our Redeemer's finished work— "Thou hast redeemed Me, O Lord, Thou that art at once My Saviour and My God."

May He grant us a keener appreciation of all that He has done for us, quickening our cold love for Him by the contemplation of His blessed Passion, and causing us to place our confidence therein for time and for eternity.

> "Behold the Lamb of God!
>   O Thou for sinners slain,
> Let it not be in vain
>   That Thou hast died :
> Thee for my Saviour let me take,
>   My only refuge let me make
> Thy piercèd side."

XVI.

THE PATH OF LIFE.

"Thou wilt shew me the path of life:
In Thy presence is fulness of joy;
In Thy right hand there are pleasures for evermore."
Ps. xvi. 11.

LAST Sunday I took for my subject the conception
of Communion with God, as we find it developed
in the Psalms. My present subject is properly an
extension of this. I wish to illustrate the manner in
which the vivid consciousness of earthly communion
with God came to form the basis of a conviction that
such communion was not to be interrupted by death;
and so paved the way for the New Testament doctrine
of a future life.

1. In the passage which I have chosen for my text,
an Old Testament saint puts into words his hopes and
aspirations for the future. It is a passage which is
very remarkable; for it seems to express, with considerable emphasis and confidence, a hope which
elsewhere in the Old Testament appears generally to
be very dim and uncertain, even if it is not lacking
altogether. We who are members of the Christian
Church are so accustomed to the doctrine of a future

resurrection and a blessed life in Heaven which is in store for God's children after death, and we regard this belief as so made sure to us by the Resurrection of our Saviour, and by His promises to all who are united to Him through faith, that we are apt to over-look the fact that this strong confidence was not and could not be shared in the same way by the saints of the Old Testament, who lived their lives before the coming of Jesus Christ to earth, and His Death and Resurrection. Before our Lord and Saviour had abolished death, and brought life and immortality to light through the Gospel, *i.e.* through His glad tidings of salvation, the doctrine of a future life could not be regarded as a certainty. It was at best a hope, an aspiration which was doubtless very dear to men's hearts, but which they scarcely ventured to put into words.

So it is that we find that even the best and holiest of men in the Old Testament often appear to be strangely despondent when they allude to the state after death, regarding it as a shadowy kind of existence which can scarcely be called life at all, in which the soul will be separated from God, and will be without hope of a brighter dawn.

Thus one Psalmist says :

> "In death there is no remembrance of Thee ;
> In the grave who shall give Thee thanks ?"
>
> (Ps. vi. 5).

Whilst another says of himself in his despair that he is—

"Cast off among the dead,
Like the slain that lie in the grave,
Whom Thou rememberest no more ;
And they are cut off from Thine hand" (Ps. lxxxviii. 5).

And later on the same poet asks mournfully :

"Wilt Thou shew wonders to the dead ?
Shall they that are deceased arise and praise Thee ?
Shall Thy loving-kindness be declared in the grave ?
Or thy faithfulness in Destruction ?
Shall Thy wonders be known in the dark ?
And Thy righteousness in the land of forgetfulness ?"
(Ps. lxxxviii. 10–12).

So, too, King Hezekiah, when he has been delivered from the fear of impending death, and granted a new lease of life on earth, exclaims, in his poem of thanksgiving :

"For the grave cannot praise Thee, death cannot celebrate Thee :
They that go down into the pit cannot hope for Thy truth,
The living, the living, he shall praise Thee, as I do this day" (Isa. xxxviii. 18, 19).

But this gloomy outlook upon the future state after death was not quite universal in Old Testament times. Here and there men seem to have risen to a faith which was able to grasp the conviction of a future blessed life with God. And the way in which they arrived at this conviction appears to have been something like this. They had attained such a real understanding, such a real grasp, of the blessedness and happiness which was theirs through communion with

God during their earthly life, that in view of this blessed union with God, and all that it meant for them, they simply overlooked the fact of death. Nothing, they felt, was able to separate them from the love of God. There was the fact of physical death, and they could not explain it away, they could not see *how* death was to be conquered. But still, they belonged to God; and God was to them their all in all. In the future, as in the present, they would still be His, come what may; and that was all their heart's desire.

I want you to notice what a very high degree of faith was involved in all this. For us, who have the privilege of living in the light of our Lord's Resurrection, the blessed hope of everlasting life has been made, as it were, so easy to grasp and to make our own. But, supposing that we were in the position of those Old Testament saints, without any direct revelation as to the conquest of death and the promise of a future life with God, I think that we should have to be living very close indeed to God here on earth to be able to rise to a sense of communion so real and definite that in face of it the dark unseen future appeared to be illuminated, and we could feel that neither life nor death, nor things present nor things to come, were able to separate us from the love of God.

Now listen to what a height of faith one of these Old Testament writers (the author of Ps. lxxiii.) rises, in the blessed sense of the reality of his communion with God. He says to his God:

"Nevertheless I am continually with Thee:
Thou hast holden my right hand.
According to Thy counsel wilt Thou lead me,
And afterward receive me gloriously.
Whom have I in heaven?
And, having Thee, there is nought that I desire upon earth.
Though my flesh and my heart should have wasted away,
God would be the Rock of my heart and my portion for
    ever."

Surely faith could scarcely make a higher venture
than this, even when guided by the full light of the
Christian revelation. "Though my flesh and my
heart should have wasted away"—even, that is, upon
the death and dissolution of my earthly frame—"God
would be the Rock of my heart and my portion for
ever." What can any one want to feel, more com-
forting, more satisfying, than this?

The same train of thought appears to have been
working in the mind of that other Psalmist, from
whom I have taken my text (the writer of Ps.
xvi.):

"Thou shalt shew me," he says, "the path of life;
In Thy presence is fulness of joy;
In Thy right hand there are pleasures for evermore."

Here the idea is the same:—felt communion with
God during this earthly life so real, so satisfying,
that it can be described as "*the path of life*," and can
be thought of as overpassing death, and lasting *for
evermore*.

2. This brings me to the point which I reached
in my sermon of last Sunday—the way in which our

Lord Jesus Christ gathered up and fulfilled in Himself the best thoughts and aspirations of the Old Testament in a higher and larger sense than they could ever have been realized by those who first gave them voice. We noticed the fact that the best of men do not always live at the same level of faith. Faith's range of vision is apt sometimes to be obscured by dark clouds; the human heart is sometimes assailed and cast down by doubting thoughts. And so these Old Testament psalmists, who were able, as we have seen, to rise upon the wings of faith, and to catch a glimpse of the real meaning of the relationship of the human soul to God, appear sometimes to have been weighed down by doubt and despondency, and to have missed the sense of the divine communion and all that it involved for them.

But with our Lord Jesus Christ this was not the case. He, as perfect Man, constantly realized, during His sinless earthly life, the highest possibilities of communion of a human soul with God the Father; and was therefore able to gather together all the lofty spiritual aspirations which found expression in the Old Testament, and to fulfil them in a far fuller and higher degree than was possible for those who first put them into words. Consequently, the words of Ps. xvi. which I have taken for my text were really fulfilled and given their perfect meaning by our Lord during His earthly life; and, when we read them, it is just as though we were reading *His* words of faith and trust in God the Father. This, we may take it,

is the justification of St. Peter's argument in his
sermon on the day of Pentecost, when he finds the
true fulfilment of the Psalmist's words in the Resurrection of Jesus Christ (Acts ii. 25 ff.).

Let us think, then, about the words of our text, as
realized by our Lord during His earthly life:

> "Thou shalt shew me the path of life:
> In Thy presence is fulness of joy;
> At Thy right hand there are pleasures for evermore."

What did "the path of life" mean for our Lord,
whilst here on earth? We can have no doubt
about it. We read the Gospels; and from beginning to end they teach us that Jesus Christ *found
the path of life to consist in the doing of the will of
God.* Think of His first recorded words when, as
a boy of twelve years old, His parents found Him
in the Temple-courts: "Wist ye not that I must
be about My Father's business?" or (as the Greek
may be more literally translated) "occupied in the
things of My Father?" (St. Luke ii. 49). And,
again, our thoughts turn at once to those words of
His to His disciples: "My meat"—*i.e.* that which
sustains and nourishes Me—"is to do the will of
Him that sent Me, and to finish His work" (St.
John iv. 34). And again and again we recall expressions which He used, such as "I must work
the works of Him that sent Me while it is day"
(St. John ix. 4). "This is the will of Him that sent
Me" (St. John vi. 39). "I do always such things as
please Him" (St. John viii. 29)—expressions which

explain His course of action during His earthly life. In fact (and we may say it with all reverence) the *leading idea* of our Lord's human life on earth was the *doing of the will of God.* During His earthly life, from His birth until the last great scene, He realized, to the fullest extent, those words of another psalmist, which are applied to Him in the Epistle to the Hebrews,

> "Then said I, Lo, I come
>
> . . .
>
> To do Thy will, O God"
>
> (Ps. xl. 7 ; Heb. x. 7).

It is in the fact that our Lord found and trod " the path of life " from the beginning of His life on earth and throughout its course, that we find the explanation of His Resurrection.

Eternal life (so He constantly tells us) is not something which lies in the future only ; it is bound up with, and realized in, the doing of the will of God here on earth, the living in close communion with Him, and growing to know Him more and more fully. " This is life eternal," He says of His disciples, " that they may know Thee, the only true God, and Jesus Christ whom Thou hast sent " (St. John xvii. 3). And again, " He that heareth My word, and believeth Him that sent Me "—*that heareth, i.e.* My message of salvation, *and believeth,* in the sense of putting himself unreservedly into the hands of God for the doing of His will, *giving himself to God*—he who does this " hath eternal life, and cometh not into judgment, but is passed out of death into life " (St. John v. 24).

Doing the will of God, then, means the present possession of eternal life : it is the treading of " the path of life " spoken of the Psalmist, and fulfilled in its highest sense by our Lord.

And *because* our Lord found, in this performance of the Father's will, the true path of life, and eternal life was thus for Him a present possession whilst living here on earth, *therefore* the Resurrection from the dead was the natural sequence ; He passed from the grave to the Resurrection of Easter Day because, as St. Peter says in that sermon of his to which I have already alluded, " it was not possible that He should be holden of death " (Acts ii. 24). That perfect communion with God the Father, which He realized during His earthly life, was something which death could not destroy. It overpassed death ; and, in so doing, broke once and for all the power of death and the grave, of sin and the Devil, and so opened the Kingdom of Heaven to all believers.

3. And for us " the path of life " is to be found through union with our Saviour, and through imitation of Him in doing always the will of God the Father. This is for us the life of communion with God, and is in very deed the beginning of eternal life here below : " Not My will, but Thine be done " ; " Thy will be done on earth, as it is in Heaven."

This path of life will lead through sorrow as well

as through joy ; it will involve that which is difficult
and painful as well as that which is joyous and con-
soling ; but we may have no doubt that it leads at
length to that fulness of joy which is in the presence
of God, and to those eternal pleasures which are in
His right hand.

XVII.

INTELLECT AND FAITH.

> " Then thought I to understand this,
> But it was too hard for me ;
> Until I went into the sanctuary of God " ;

or, more accurately :

> " And I kept thinking how to understand this ;
> It was vain labour in my eyes ;
> Until I went into the sanctuary of God."
>
> Ps. lxxiii. 16, 17*a*.

THE poet is here concerned with a problem which only emerged at a relatively late period in the history of Israel. The difficulty of believing in God's righteous government of the world, in face of the apparent prosperity of the wicked man and the adversity of the good man, seems not to have pressed itself upon men's minds with any special cogency, until a severe crisis in the national life had made separation between class and class, and tested Jehovah's servants in the glowing furnace of affliction.

In the early and middle days of the Judæan monarchy, when the power of the nation was at its zenith, and men enjoyed, upon the whole, happy and prosperous times, it was the commonly received theory that in this life Jehovah rewarded the righteous and punished the wicked; prosperity was regarded as an immediate mark of His favour; adversity—especially if sudden and overwhelming—as a sure sign of His displeasure.

But the period of decadence which preceded the fall of the kingdom of Judah was marked by grave social abuses and growing indifference to the spirit of Jehovah's religion, coupled with bare formalism or the definite introduction of foreign cults. Upright and pious men formed a despised, if not a persecuted, minority; justice and virtue seemed to bring, not success, but loss and failure in their train.

And during the Babylonian Exile this condition of things appears rather to have been accentuated than diminished. The bulk of the people accommodated itself very easily to its new circumstances, and adopted to a great extent the customs of the nation in the midst of which it was placed. Those who clung to the faith of Israel, and, keeping steadfastly in view the possibility of a restoration, made it their aim to preserve their individuality as a nation and as a religious community, were but the few among the many—an insignificant party exciting generally the scorn and hatred of their fellows. Jehovah's Servant, spoken of in the later chapters of Isaiah as the object of shame and spitting, as misunderstood, oppressed, and even done to death on account of the attitude which he adopted, represents, in the first instance, this small body in the midst of the nation, and sets forward, doubtless, a true picture of the sufferings which it was forced to undergo.

Nor was the return from Babylon by any means a restoration of happy and prosperous times for this faithful remnant. Though those who availed themselves of the decree of Cyrus belonged, in the main, to the body who held by the hope of Israel, and were, as a whole, animated by a common aim, yet the hardships to be contended with were enormous; weakness and poverty within, oppression and opposition from without, raised up a series of difficulties which nothing but the untiring energy and faith of the more patriotic spirits were able to surmount.

It was in times such as these that men turned to review their ancient position, and to perceive its partiality and insufficiency. Righteousness certainly no longer appeared uniformly to bring its reward, nor wickedness its due punishment. We must recollect that at that stage of thought quick returns were looked for. The doctrine of a future life after death had not yet been developed in Israel's religion. The soul was thought of as living on, indeed, in the unseen world, but in a state of existence which could scarcely be spoken of as life, far removed from all human interests and the hope of a brighter dawn.[1] The view that righteousness would be rewarded after death, and that present hardship might form a training for a future state, so far from being generally held, was, in fact, the outcome of thought which appeared *later*

[1] See, further, Sermon No. XVI, p. 197.

14

on as part of the answer to the difficulties which the anomalies of the present life excited in men's minds. But before such a stage had been reached it may well be understood that to men who lived in the expectation of the immediate vindication of Jehovah's righteous government, many serious stumbling-blocks to faith would present themselves.

And it was this question—the same that aroused the passionate expostulation of Jeremiah at the close of the monarchy (Jer. xii. 1–3), or later called forth the careful and detailed treatment of the author of the Book of Job—which exercised the mind of the writer of our Psalm, and at first seemed likely to prove fatal to his belief in God's good providence.

We hear first of all how critical was the position of his faith for the time being:

"But as for me, my feet were almost gone:
  My steps had well-nigh slipped,
  For I was envious of the arrogant,
  When I saw the prosperity of the wicked."

And then he goes on to set forth in some detail the position of these unrighteous men.   To his imagination they seem to escape all the ills of life and to enjoy its good things, while all the time they laugh God to scorn.   Bitterly, in conclusion, he contrasts their position with his own:

"Behold, these men are ungodly,
  And, secure for ever, they have won great substance.
  Surely in vain have I cleansed my heart,
  And washed my hands in innocency.
  And yet I was plagued all the day,
  And my rebuke came every morning."

But even in his misery it comes upon him that this is not the attitude which a member of the true Israel ought to adopt. Such hopeless abandonment is, in fact, a denial of his belief, a proving false to the cause of which he stands as the representative.

> " If I had said, I will speak thus,
> Behold, I should have been a traitor to the generation
> of thy children."

Therefore, when faith seems weakest, he determines to make the severest trial of faith. He takes his difficulty into the sanctuary of God, the place which was regarded as the seat of God's earthly government, the House of Prayer in which devout men were wont to see Jehovah's power and glory, and so the right spot for seeking enlightenment at such a spiritual crisis. And it is here that a solution offers itself to his mind, and he meets with perfect satisfaction.

> " And I kept thinking how to understand this ;
> It was vain labour in my eyes :
> Until I went into the sanctuary of God,
> And gave heed unto their latter end."

Let us glance for a moment at the Psalmist's explanation. It is briefly this. The prosperity of the ungodly is, after all, more apparent than real. There is a Nemesis who is waiting in their path. Even while they stretch out their eager hands to gather life's flowers, the solid rock gives way beneath their feet, and they go down quick into the abyss :

> "Surely in slippery places dost Thou set them,
> Thou castest them down into ruins;
> How are they become a desolation in a moment,
> Swept off, consumed by terrors!
> As a dream, when one has awakened,
> So, Lord, when Thou arousest thyself, Thou shalt
>   despise their semblance.
> Oh, that my heart should be embittered,
> And that I should be pierced in my reins!
> I indeed was brutish and ignorant,
> I was like a beast before Thee."

Now it must be observed that this solution is not in any sense final and altogether satisfactory. It represents a small advance in thought upon the old opinion; but is in fact merely a partial and fragmentary contribution to the truth, and was destined soon to be merged in a larger view of God's dealings with men.

But this is not the Psalmist's real gain during his visit to the sanctuary. We find it rather in that conviction which seizes him of the great reality of his communion with God—a conviction which calls forth from him such a confession of trust in God as forms, when we consider his partial light and uncertain knowledge of the future life, a passage as remarkable and splendid as anything in the pages of the Old Testament.

> "Nevertheless, I am continually with Thee;
> Thou hast holden my right hand,
> According to Thy counsel wilt Thou lead me,
> And afterward receive me gloriously.
> Whom have I in heaven?
> And, having Thee, there is nought that I desire upon earth
> Though my flesh and my heart should have wasted away,
> God would be the Rock of my heart and my portion for ever.

It has been much questioned whether the Psalmist is here formulating any definite statement of belief in a life of blessedness beyond the grave. This does not seem to be precisely the position which he takes. Rather, in the fulness of the sense of his communion with Jehovah, he ignores or overlooks the fact of death; feeling that he possesses all he needs, and that, in any event, he is entirely in the hands, and under the special care, of his God.

And we do not ask whether he was ever again troubled with doubts as to God's providence. He may indeed have found occasion to modify and enlarge his rational view of the question which had troubled his mind. But of that grasp wherewith he tells us that God holds his right hand we feel sure that he never more lost touch; and this, we may believe, was sufficient to carry him through his life, up to, and past, the gates of death.

I wish to dwell briefly, not so much upon the particular difficulty which assailed the Psalmist's faith, as upon the attitude which he adopted in dealing with it. In face of such a problem, there are two other positions which conceivably he might have taken up. He might have argued that the question was dangerous, as striking at the foundations of belief, and so have determined to preserve his faith by ignoring it, and as far as possible putting it out of mind. Or, on the other hand, he might have reasoned that, until such a difficulty had been set at rest, belief reposed

upon too precarious a basis, and that it was better
therefore to suspend his judgment, together with the
worship of a God whose dealings with mankind were
so mysterious and obscure.

He did neither. Rather, while maintaining and
exercising his right to rational investigation of the
question which harassed his mind, in the light of the
facts which lay to his hand, he trusted that beyond
this there was something *supernatural* which God
alone was able to grant in response to an act of faith ;
and that this latter, so far from being antagonistic to
the results obtained by the exercise of reason, was
indeed intended to condition and to set them in a
right direction.

And so he betook himself to the place where God's
mysterious Presence was believed specially to be
manifest, and staking all upon an act of faith, he
obtained, not merely a rational solution of his
difficulty, but, what was of far higher value, such an
inward sense of Jehovah's Fatherly care and protec-
tion as secured him for ever in his faith and endued
him with perfect peace.

And this is surely the way in which we ought to
meet the doubts and difficulties which so frequently
assail us. We are not likely to place them on one
side and to ignore them, but we must feel bound to
subject them to the searching light which the advance-
ment of knowledge has placed within our reach.
Rightly so. But let us not forget that we are
members of a Church which believes in and proclaims

the supernatural Presence of her Lord in her midst, and that He has promised to give *Himself* to those who seek Him, in order that He may guide them into all truth. And let us be willing at least to *make trial* of the act of faith, coming to Him that we may cast our burdens upon Him, and receive for ourselves out of His fulness.

Not alone the Hebrew poet, but ten thousand others in all ages, will assure us that we shall not be disappointed; for these all have sought God in His sanctuary, and have set to their seal that He is true.

And as we thus draw near to place ourselves in personal contact with Him who is at once our Brother, our Saviour, and our God, we shall know that we have proved the truth of the Psalmist's witness, and shall be able with him to say:

"But as for me, it is good for me to draw nigh to God:
I have made the Lord God my refuge,
That I may tell of all Thy works."

XVIII.

PROPOSALS OF CONVOCATION FOR THE EXPURGATION OF THE PRAYER-BOOK PSALTER.

" The righteous shall rejoice when he seeth the vengeance :
He shall wash his footsteps in the blood of the ungodly.
So that a man shall say, Verily there is a reward for the
righteous:
Doubtless there is a God that judgeth the earth."

Ps. lviii. 9, 10.

I SUPPOSE that there never was a time, within the
experience of this generation, when the abiding
spiritual value of the Book of Psalms has shone out
more clearly than it does to-day in the midst of the
present stress and trouble.   It is to the Psalms that we
turn instinctively in order to express and to interpret
our own inmost thoughts and feelings.   The human soul
whose experiences are depicted there ; who sinks into
the deep mire and is all but submerged beneath the
rushing waters ; over whose head the billows break as
with a loud cry for help he stretches out despairing
hands and grasps the rock, which, beyond all human
hope, is *there* just when it is most needed ; who is
drawn out by some unseen Power, and feels his feet
once more upon the firm ground ; who is this but *our
own soul*, true to the life in every detail, a moving

photograph, as it were, of all our alternating spiritual moods and vicissitudes ?

If we reflect upon it for a moment, it must, from the human point of view, seem to us an amazing thing that poets like the Psalmists, who lived their lives more than two thousand years ago, and who were, in addition, separated from us by that deep cleavage which must always divide the thought of the East from that of the West, should have passed through spiritual experiences which seem to have been, in all respects, akin to our own ; should have clothed those experiences in words which strike a responsive chord in our own hearts at the present day ; *and* should have tapped, as it were, a source of comfort which is ever-flowing, ever-fresh, as real and as satisfying to us in England to-day as it was those many hundred years ago in far-distant Palestine.

How do we account for it ? I can offer only one explanation. It belongs to what we rightly describe as the *Inspiration* of the Bible. It is the witness of the human consciousness to a Power outside itself, invisible yet very near, offering Itself to be found by those who seek It in sincerity and truth, and, when found, abundantly satisfying. And this source of spiritual strength and comfort is the same for all ages, for it is the well-spring of life-eternal.

> " Our fathers hoped in Thee ;
> They trusted in Thee, and Thou didst deliver them.
> They called upon Thee, and were holpen :
> They put their trust in Thee, and were not confounded "
> (Ps. xxii. 4, 5).

Now for many years past the two Houses of Convocation of Canterbury, *i.e.* the two great representative bodies of the southern half of our Church of England, have had in hand the very difficult, yet, in many respects, most necessary task of preparing a scheme of revision for our Book of Common Prayer. Just recently, they have had before them the question of the revision of the Lectionary, *i.e.* they have been reviewing the selection of chapters appointed to be read in church as First and Second Lessons; and in the selection of these lessons—and, especially, of the Sunday Lessons—they have suggested many improvements. Together with this there has come up the question of the recitation of the Psalms in public worship; and here also certain suggestions have been made. One at least of these seems to require very careful discussion and explanation before it is adopted. There are a certain number of Psalms and Psalm-passages which are commonly known as *Imprecatory*, because that in them the Psalmists, in the face of flagrant wickedness which seems at the time at which they speak, to be flourishing unchecked, invoke the wrath of the righteous God upon evil-doers, or view their impending punishment with unfeigned satisfaction. It is urged that passages such as these are contrary to the Christian ideal as set forth in the life and teaching of our Lord; and therefore it is proposed, not merely to omit them from use in public worship, Sunday and week-day alike, but also to exclude them altogether from the Prayer-Book

Psalter, their omission being indicated in the printed text by the use of asterisks. The passages in question are Ps. lviii. as a whole (the Psalm from which our text is taken), and single verses, or groups of verses, from eight other Psalms.[1]

We have here — it will be noticed — a rather remarkable coincidence. For years we have been repeating these imprecatory passages in the monthly round, and probably they have not made any very deep impression upon most of us; since, thank God, we do not in normal times have to deal with cruel, malignant, and treacherous foes. Present circumstances, however, have, as we have already remarked, brought the Psalms much more nearly home to us as the living expression of our own inward experience; and, among other aspects, we undoubtedly begin to understand—even if we do not enter into—the spirit which actuated the Psalmists in their denunciations of the wicked. It is merely an accident that the part of the Prayer-Book revision which deals with the Psalms happens to have come before Convocation during war-time, and so, by coincidence, at the very time when the imprecatory passages have come to have a real meaning for us, it is proposed to omit them from public worship altogether as alien to the spirit of Christianity.

Let us now consider the justification of this pro-

---

[1] Ps. lv. 16, 24, 25, lxviii. 21–23, lix. 23–29, cix. 5–19, cxxxvii. 7–9, cxxxix. 19–22, cxl. 9, 10, cxliii. 12 (adding the final words " for I am Thy servant " to ver. 11).

posal, and endeavour (so far as we may in a short time) to assess its soundness.

The fact that the religious teaching of the Old Testament is in many respects rudimentary and defective as compared with that of the New Testament, is a fact which is directly attested by the New Testament itself. According to the opening words of the writer of the Epistle to the Hebrews, God spake in time past unto the fathers in the prophets "by divers portions and in divers manners"; and he contrasts this partial and imperfect revelation, conveyed in different modes, with the full and final revelation made by Jesus Christ: "at the end of these days He hath spoken unto us in His Son."

It was, you will notice, a genuinely *divine* revelation which was made to Israel in Old Testament times; it was *God Himself* who spake in time past unto the fathers in the prophets; *but* this revelation was partial, fragmentary, gradual, conveyed to its recipients not, as it were, in a flash, but bit by bit and through the imperfect agency of human media. "Holy men of God spake as they were moved by the Holy Ghost" (2 St. Pet. i. 21); but, inasmuch as they were themselves human, they were liable to the defects of humanity, and the message which they were divinely inspired to convey was often imperfectly apprehended, and was set, as it were, in a frame which was inwrought with the imperfection of human thought and passion. Thus, when at length it pleased God to speak unto mankind in the Person of His Son, we find that the scattered rays of the twilight of revelation are absorbed in the full light of the one bright beam, and the shadows disappear.

And so our Lord, in His teaching, at times draws attention to imperfections in the teaching of the Old Testament, and claims to supersede them—most notably in the very question which at present concerns us, the attitude which we ought to adopt in relation to our enemies: " Ye have heard that it was said, Thou shalt love thy neighbour, and hate thine enemy : but I say unto you, Love your enemies, and pray for them that persecute you; that ye may be sons of your Father which is in heaven : for He maketh His sun to rise on the evil and the good, and sendeth rain on the just and the unjust " (St. Matt. v. 43 ff.).

Taking it, then, to be a well-established fact that the Old Testament, as the record of an evolution or gradual growth in religious faith, contains much that was destined to be superseded by the teaching of our Lord, it has still to be proved that the attitude adopted towards the wicked in the Psalms which we are considering necessarily falls within this category. Indeed, there are certain weighty considerations which may well give us pause before we pronounce such a verdict. For example: it is clear that of the whole Old Testament the Psalms and the Prophets stand out most prominently as of the highest spiritual and moral worth. Of these two divisions,

again, it is undoubtedly the Psalms which grip us
most closely; the reason being that, while the
Prophets are preachers of righteousness to their own
nation or to the world at large, the Psalmists, for the
most part, deal with *personal* religion, and set before
us the outpourings of individual souls in communion
with their God. Now every one must surely admit
that the spiritual level of the personal religion which
we find in the Psalms is an extraordinarily high one.
That thirsting after God, that staking of all hopes
on Him, and the finding of one's sole good in His
society, that rising on the wings of faith into a serener
and purer atmosphere, where the dark clouds of
earth seem to sink out of sight below and nothing
intervenes to dim the sunshine of God's presence—
this all represents a grade of spiritual attainment
which offers us an imperishable *ideal*, the unique
value of which lies largely in the fact that it *is* an
ideal to which few even of the best of us can wholly
attain. Our Lord Himself found in the Psalms the
fitting medium for the expression of His deepest soul-
outpourings in communion with God the Father;
and two out of His seven last "words" from the
Cross—"My God, My God, why hast Thou forsaken
Me?" and "Into Thy hands I commend My spirit"
—were drawn directly from the Psalms (Ps. xxii. 1,
xxxi. 5), showing how accurately they served to
voice the inmost movements of His human soul
even at the crisis of His earthly life. This being so,
can it be claimed to be an altogether satisfactory

explanation of the presence of imprecatory passages in the Psalms, if we say that they represent an imperfect stage of morality which has been abrogated by the Christian dispensation ? If, on the one hand, the Psalmists rise high above us in their spirituality, in their realization of all that religion is capable of meaning, does it seem likely that, on the other hand (*i.e.* in regard to this question which is now exercising our minds), they fall far below our standard ?

Of course, it may be answered that the Book of Psalms is not a unity ; that we have in it the work of a multitude of authors, and that we can distinguish grades of spirituality in Psalm as compared with Psalm almost as clearly as we can distinguish grades of poetic beauty and skilful technique. This, of course, is true to a large extent ; yet it remains the fact that there is about the Book as a whole a large amount of solidarity ; and so far from its being an easy matter to separate the lofty spiritual passages from the imprecatory passages, and to claim that the authors of the former would not have endorsed the latter, we can, in some cases at least, adduce concrete instances in which the two kinds of passage occur together in the same Psalm. A partial solution of this apparent antithesis is doubtless to be found in the fact that, the clearer the realization of the beauty of holiness, the sharper necessarily is the recoil from all that is by nature opposed to the ideal of holiness.

"O ye that love the Lord, see that ye hate the thing that is evil" (Ps. xcvii. 10).

If our thirst for God, our dependence upon Him, approached more closely to the ideal set forth in the Psalms, is it not certain that our antipathy to all that is base and evil would be more vigorously expressed in word and deed?

Now let us turn to consider very briefly the attitude which our Lord would have us adopt in relation to our enemies. The subject is, in many respects, a very difficult one. There are different statements in the New Testament which it is not altogether easy to correlate; and so, anything that I can say must be taken largely as a personal opinion and subject to correction, except in so far as it is supported by the warrant of Holy Scripture.

It will help us if we begin by making a classification of the people whom we understand by the term "enemy." There are, in the first place, *personal enemies*, *i.e.* individuals with whom any one of us as an individual may have some cause of feud. And, secondly, there are *enemies of society in the aggregate*. This latter class we may subdivide into (*a*) *individuals*, such as notorious criminals, whose misdeeds form a menace to the stability of civilized society, and therefore ordinarily bring them within the clutches of the law; and, again, (*b*) *groups of individuals*, such as *nations*, with whom we as a nation may be engaged in hostilities. We think, of course, of our own national foes at the present time, and, in particular, of the German nation.

Now it seems to be clear that, when our Lord, in the Sermon on the Mount, says, "Love your enemies," and when, in the same discourse, He uses the familiar words about turning the other cheek, He is referring solely to the ideal of conduct at which we as individuals should aim in relation to our *personal enemies*. Witness His own conduct when suffering the insults, invectives, and assaults which He underwent at His trial: "Who, when He was reviled, reviled not again; when He suffered, He threatened not; but committed Himself to Him that judgeth righteously" (1 St. Pet. ii. 23). These were injuries which, if we may say so with all reverence, affected only His own dignity, infringed only His personal rights, inflicted suffering upon Him as an individual. And here, beyond all manner of doubt, He holds up before us a great Ideal, which, as Christians, we are bound to imitate to the best of our powers. "Christ also suffered for you, leaving you an example, that ye should follow His steps" (1 St. Pet. ii. 21).

Take two types of conduct under personal injury, and contrast them. The first comes from the Old Testament. You doubtless remember how, when the queen Athaliah effected the massacre of all the seed royal of the kingdom of Judah, and seized the crown, the good old priest Jehoiada managed to conceal the infant Joash, brought him up in secret, and then, producing him at the fitting moment, succeeded in dethroning Athaliah, and in establishing the rightful heir upon the throne. The Book of Chronicles tells

15

us that Joash served God as long as Jehoiada lived to
instruct him ; but after his death he was perverted by
his courtiers and turned aside after the service of
idols. Zechariah, the son of Jehoiada, boldly pro-
tested against this defection from Jehovah ; and the
result was that he was stoned to death. " Thus,"
says the narrator, " Joash the king remembered not
the kindness which Jehoiada his father had done to
him, but slew his son. And when he died, he said,
" The Lord look upon it, and require it " (2 Chron.
xxiv. 22).

Now turn to the narrative of another stoning.
" They stoned Stephen, calling upon the Lord, and
saying, Lord Jesus, receive my spirit. And he
kneeled down, and cried with a loud voice, Lord,
lay not this sin to their charge. And when he had
said this, he fell asleep " (Acts vii. 59 f.).

We cannot blame Zechariah. He does not seem to
have resisted. We do not read that he hurled curses
and invectives against his cruel murderers. He only
committed the judgment of them to the righteous
God. Yet we cannot doubt that it is the example
of St. Stephen, who interceded for his murderers, and
not the example of Zechariah, that has proved fruitful
in the regeneration of humanity.

We cannot, for lack of time, deal with other
passages in our Lord's teaching which speak of the
forgiveness of personal enemies. What I want you
now to notice is that there was a class of opponents
to our Lord during His earthly life whom He regarded

with a spirit which was very far removed from the spirit of forgiveness. We read that He assailed the scribes and Pharisees in terms of invective: "Ye serpents! ye generation of vipers! how can ye escape the damnation of hell?" (St. Matt. xxiii. 33). The reason for this is clear. Here was a body of men who were opposed to our Lord *on account of His teaching*; their whole aim was to thwart the growth of the divine Society which He came to earth to found; in the face of evident proof that His teaching came from God, they resolutely closed their eyes, and ascribed it to the Devil. They were the enemies of Society in the most flagrant sense, inasmuch as, in face of the light, they set themselves to oppose the greatest social movement for the regeneration of mankind that the world has ever known. There is a sin against the Holy Ghost which has no forgiveness, "neither in this world, neither in the world to come" (St. Matt. xii. 31–32).

We are, I believe, gravely in error if we suppose that our Lord's words, "Father, forgive them, for they know not what they do," refer to this class of men. They seem properly to refer to the Roman soldiers who, in nailing Him to the Cross, were merely performing their work in carrying out (as they supposed) the execution of a malefactor; and may we claim, please God, that they refer to us, when in our ignorance and frailty we all unwittingly nail Him to the Cross again?

Now take our own attitude towards an individual

enemy of society—let us say, a murderer. From time to time we read in the papers the account of a shocking murder, the details of which almost make our blood run cold, so hateful and horrible does it seem that such fiends in human shape should exist. It may be, perhaps, that, though the guilt of the prisoner is morally certain, there seems a possibility of a flaw in the evidence which may lead to the murderer's acquittal; and we hold our breath, as it were, till we read that the guilt has been definitely proved, and the judge has passed sentence of death, and then we are relieved, and, we may almost say, *glad*—sick at heart, indeed, that such wickedness should exist, but glad that justice has taken its course, since our whole conscience cries out that this is the only penalty which fits the crime, and that it is a blessed thing that the world is to be purged of such a criminal. We should not, I take it, be wrong if we were to make it a matter of prayer that justice should be divinely aided in taking its due course; and then we should, in fact, be making use of imprecation against the murderer, very much as the Psalmists did.

Observe that we are not dealing with the future of the criminal's soul beyond the veil; we leave that in the hand of God. Only we are concerned that justice should have its course in this present world, and that thus *God's righteousness*, upon which the whole framework of true civilization is founded, should be vindicated.

And so with a criminal nation which has violated every law of God and of civilized humanity. Our vindictiveness against Germany — I use the term "vindictiveness" deliberately in its proper sense of a desire for vengeance, or the execution of justice— is not of a personal character. Those of us who have lost relations and friends—and who has not?— do not feel vindictive, I take it, because these have fallen on the field of honour. That which makes our blood boil if we have any spark of true humanity is the long list of terrible crimes committed chiefly against members of nations other than our own who are our allies; and is there any need to maintain that according to the Biblical, the Christian, standard, this is a feeling which is wholly noble? We cannot put aside these crimes, which if they flourished unchecked or unpunished would make the world a hell, and consent to shake the blood-stained hands of a nation which shows no sign of repentance, no movement towards reparation. Readiness to forgive an un-repentant enemy for hideous crimes committed against other people is in no sense a Christian virtue; and the fact that we may feel ready to do this does not argue that we have attained a high standard of Christian ethics, but rather the reverse.

A few last words as to the Imprecatory Psalms. I feel assured that many of the passages in question have to do with a situation like that which confronts us to-day. Some of them have indeed been super-

seded owing to the fact that we no longer hold the
Old Testament theory which involved the sinner's
relatively innocent family in his own guilt. I can feel
no doubt that, for example, Pss. cxxxvii. and cix. should
be expurgated for use in public worship, or omitted
altogether.[1] God forbid that we should wish to take
the German children, and to dash them against the
stones ; nor can we use such imprecations as

> "Let his children be vagabonds, and beg their bread ;
> Let them be driven out of their desolate homes.
>
> .   .   .   .
>
> Let there be no man to pity him,
> Nor to have compassion upon his fatherless children.
> Let his posterity be destroyed :
> In the next generation let his name be clean put out."

But look for a moment at Ps. lviii., from which our text
is taken, and which is the only Psalm which it is
proposed should wholly disappear.

> "Break their teeth, O God, in their mouths ;
> Smite the jaw-bones of the lions, O Lord."

This is an imprecation to which exception is taken.
But no one, surely, would interpret this literally in
reference to a cruel act of mutilation to be inflicted
upon individuals. We should be breaking the teeth
of the German lion if by a successful air-raid we
damaged the munition-works at Essen ; and our Navy
does it when it sends the U-boats, one after another,
to the bottom. The following verses are obscure in
detail ; but their general drift is that they pray

[1] See, on these Psalms, p. 142.

God to bring to nought the best-laid schemes of the foe.

Then we come to the words of our text:

> "The righteous shall rejoice when he seeth the vengeance:
> He shall wash his footsteps in the blood of the ungodly."

We open our papers, as we did a short while back, and read that the British armies have advanced 3000 yards along a ten-mile front; and we thank God. This is a consummation for which we have been hoping and praying. Could a poet—a *poet*, mind you —whose whole art it is to sketch a picture with a few bold strokes, have suggested what must be the character of such an advance more realistically? Such realism may shock the susceptibilities of comfortable critics who sit at home in their arm-chairs; but we cannot on their account make the Bible a pacifist book, or expunge from it all passages which paint the divine vengeance in terrible colours. For there follows immediately the justification:

> "So that a man shall say, Verily there is a reward
> for the righteous:
> Doubtless there is a God that judgeth the earth."

The vindication of the divine government of the world—that is a consummation which our brave soldiers, who rejoice when they see the vengeance, have closely at heart, whether they would express it in so many words or not; and it is a consummation for which we all devoutly pray.

XIX.

GOD OUR REFUGE AND STRENGTH.

" God is our hope and strength :
A very present help in trouble."—Ps. xlvi. 1.

I HAVE made the experiment of translating this
splendid Psalm into a form which reproduces,
as nearly as is possible, the rhythm of the original
Hebrew.   In the Psalms, as also in a great part of the
writings of the Prophets, there is poetry in the noble
thoughts, nobly expressed ; there is poetry in the
parallelism, *i.e.* in the way in which the second clause
of a couplet answers to the first, often reiterating its
thought in varied language, and thus interpreting and
emphasizing it ; there is poetry, again, in the chaste
and vigorous language of our English Versions,
especially in the Prayer-Book Version of the Psalms,
which is derived from the translation of Coverdale.
What we miss, however, in the English versions as
compared with the Hebrew, is the *rhythm* of the
original, which is not only a thing of beauty in itself,
but also serves to give due stress and balance to the
thoughts contained in the Psalm, and thus to help in
its interpretation.

I say *rhythm* rather than *metre*, because the Hebrew system of poetry is not strictly metrical, *i.e.* not a matter of counting so many syllables to the line, but rather a matter of reckoning so many stress-accents or rhythmical beats, the intervening unstressed syllables varying in number in different lines, but the whole effect being one of poetic uniformity of structure which is satisfying to the artistic sense. This form of poetical composition is not confined to Hebrew, but has sometimes been employed in English poetry, especially in some of the oldest English poems which are known to us. Its existence in Hebrew is a comparatively modern discovery—in fact it cannot even now be said to have gained universal recognition among scholars, though those who have closely studied the subject are agreed upon it. The Psalm of which we are speaking happens to be a very complete and clear illustration of its use. In it we find, as a rule, four rhythmical beats to the line, varied by couplets of three beats to the line which mark the close of a stanza or strophe. That the Psalm was intended to fall into such stanzas is further proved by the occurrence, at each such point, of the Hebrew term *Selah*, a musical note indicating, almost certainly, an *interlude*, when the singing ceased and the instruments struck up in a louder refrain. The *Selah* is omitted in the Prayer-Book Version, but you will find it in the Authorized and Revised Versions.

In order to bring out this rhythm with as close an

approximation to the Hebrew as is possible, I
translate the Psalm thus:

"Gód is for ús   a réfuge and stréngth,
A hélp in troúbles   próved full wéll :
Therefóre fear we nót   though the eárth be móved,
Though the moúntains subsíde in the heárt of the séa.
            Its wáters ráge and fóam ;
            The moúntains quáke at its swélling.

There's a ríver whose stréams make glád the cíty ;
By thém the Most Hígh   has hállowed His abóde.[1]
Gód is in her mídst,   she shall nót be móved ;
Gód shall hélp her   at the túrn of the mórning.
Nátions róar,   kíngdoms sháke ;
He útters His vóice,   the eárth dissólves.
        The Lórd of hósts is wíth us ;
        Our strónghold is Jácob's Gód.

Cóme, behóld   the wórks of the Lórd,
Hów He has sét   dismáy on the eárth :
Abólishing wárs,   to the boúnds of the eárth,
The bów He breáks,   and snáps the speár,
        The wággons He búrns in the fíre.

Desíst, and knów   that Í am Gód :
I will be exálted among the I will be exálted in the
    nátions,   eárth.
        The Lórd of hósts is wíth us ;
        Our strónghold is Jácob's Gód."

---

[1] The Hebrew text of this couplet, represented in Revised Version by
the rendering,

"There is a river, the streams whereof make glad the city of God,
    The holy place of the tabernacles of the Most High,"

contains 5 + 3 rhythmical beats, instead of 4 + 4. Our emendation
takes over the last stress-word of line 1, אֱלֹהִים, "God," to the
beginning of line 2, reading it as אֱלֵיהֶם, "By them" (the streams).
The rest of the line is emended in accordance with the Greek version,
which presupposes a very trifling change in the Hebrew consonants.

As regards the historical occasion of our Psalm it is impossible to speak with certainty, though we *can* speak with a considerable degree of probability.   In attempting to settle the date and occasion of particular Psalms we have very little to guide us.   The historical notes prefixed to some of the Psalms are much later than the Psalms themselves.   They represent merely the guess-work of Jewish scribes, who had not more to guide them than we have ourselves; and in many cases they are plainly unsuitable to the contents of the Psalm to which they refer.   From the nature of most of the Psalms historical allusions are scanty, or altogether lacking.   Where we can venture an opinion at all, the most that we can usually do is to say that a particular Psalm would suit a particular occasion : it is only very rarely, if ever, that we can maintain that a Psalm *must* have been called forth by a particular set of circumstances, because our knowledge of large tracts of Hebrew history is very fragmentary, and there may have been other unrecorded occasions to which a Psalm in question may have been equally, or more, suitable.   With regard to Ps. xlvi. we can maintain this much—that it seems altogether suitable to the historical events of which we read two Sundays ago in the First Lessons at Mattins and Evensong, the invasion of Judah by the Assyrian king, Sennacherib, and the disaster to his army which obliged him to abandon his campaign and retreat into his own country, leaving Jerusalem free and uncaptured, in accordance with the prediction of the prophet Isaiah.

The vivid and picturesque narrative of 2 Kings xviii. and xix. must be so familiar to you that I need not enlarge upon it.[1] The account of the campaign is supplemented, and largely corroborated, by Sennacherib's own account which we find in his Annals, written on a clay cylinder which is now in the British Museum. The fact that some great disaster, such as is mentioned in the Biblical narrative, overtook the Assyrian army is very naturally not recorded by Sennacherib; but it is noteworthy that, while he makes the most of the heavy tribute which he exacted from Hezekiah in the first instance, and the cities which he captured, and tells us that he shut up Hezekiah in Jerusalem "like a bird in a cage," he makes no allusion to the capture of Jerusalem; and such an omission would be quite inconceivable if he had succeeded in his undertaking. The Assyrians were in the habit of magnifying their successes, and concealing their disasters.

A quaint corroboration of the Assyrian disaster comes to us from the Greek historian Herodotus. Herodotus relates a tradition which he heard when he was in Egypt, to the effect that, when Sennacherib was advancing through Palestine against Egypt, the King of Egypt made supplication to his god Hephæstus, and in answer to his prayer the god sent a swarm of field-mice, which came by night upon the Assyrian host, and while they were sleeping gnawed through their bow-strings and the leathern handles of their shields, so that in the morning they found them-

[1] See pp. 113 ff.

selves defenceless, and were obliged to beat a hasty retreat. In proof of the truth of this story, Herodotus states that he saw in Egypt a statue of the god Hephæstus, holding a mouse in his hand, with underneath it the inscription, " Look on me, and learn to reverence the gods." [1]

We need not hesitate in concluding that, of the two stories, the Bible-story, which is simpler, is nearer to the truth. Probably the visitation of the angel of Jehovah was a sudden pestilence, of which in the Greek story the mice are symbolical, or with which they may actually have been connected, just as, in the account of the capture of the Ark by the Philistines in the days of Eli, we find that mice or rats are connected with the bubonic plague which decimated the Philistine cities. That the parasites of rats act as carriers of this plague is now a well-ascertained scientific fact.

Here we have a natural explanation of the catastrophe, but this does not in the slightest degree diminish its miraculous character as a signal proof of the Divine intervention. God acts, as a rule, through natural agencies. The proof of His working is seen in the raising up of the agency to meet a particular crisis, which, from the human point of view, might seem to be beyond remedy. It is, in this sense, surely a miracle that the huge German army, carefully trained and equipped after a preparation of more than forty years, should have been met and held by our

[1] Herodotus, ii. 141.

"contemptible little army," and that our army should have grown, beyond all human expectation, to be the tremendous instrument which it now is. "Out of weakness they were made strong, waxed mighty in war, turned to flight armies of aliens."

Now let us briefly examine our Psalm. Was it written in the calm after the storm, when Jehovah's mighty deliverance had taken effect; or actually during the period of stress, with the full prophetic insight which Isaiah exhibited in face of the same crisis? We cannot say for certain. In any case what strikes us most is the fulness of calm trust and confidence in God which the poet exhibits. God is for him, and for all who share his faith,

"A help in troubles proved full well."

This is no mere aspiration. He *knows* it to be a *fact.* God has been proved in the past; He is being proved now; He will be proved in the future; and will *never* fail those who take refuge in Him. That is the Psalmist's faith, and it is the kind of faith which can enable a man, or a nation, to carry on, and to win through in face of troubles as dark as those which we are now experiencing.

"Therefore fear we not though the earth be moved, Though the mountains subside in the heart of the sea."

Could any metaphor express more vividly the convulsions through which the world is passing at the present? Yet, says the Psalmist, "We fear not."

Then, turning a moment, he contemplates the vision of the raging sea which he has conjured up :

> " Its waters rage and foam ;
> The mountains quake at its swelling."

It is a terrific spectacle; yet, as a fact, we know that all this elemental rage and fury, this apparently resistless might, is curbed and controlled by God. We think of that grand passage from the Book of Jeremiah which came in this morning's lesson : " Fear ye not Me ? saith the Lord : will ye not tremble at My presence, which have placed the sand for the bound of the sea by a perpetual decree, that it cannot pass it : and though the waves thereof toss themselves, yet can they not prevail; though they roar, yet can they not pass over it ? " (Jer. v. 22). This is true, we know, of the blind force which impels the ocean to rage and strive to break its bounds, yet all in vain ; are we to think that it is less true of the like blind force which sets a nation to lift itself in overweening arrogance, and to strive against God and His holy laws ?

Here the stanza ends ; and in the next stanza, in striking contrast, we pass at once to a scene of the calmest peace and joy :

> " There's a river whose streams   make glad the city ;
>   By them the Most High   has hallowed His abode.
>   God is in her midst,   she shall not be moved ;
>   God shall help her   at the turn of the morning."

The city is Jerusalem ; but what, we may ask, is the meaning of the river ? Jerusalem, set high among her

bare and arid hills, possesses no river or stream. All
that she has in the way of living water, as distinct
from water stored in reservoirs and cisterns, is the
single small spring of Gihon, the modern St. Mary's
fountain. This issues from the steep side of the hill
on which the ancient city of David or fortress of
Zion (the old Jebusite stronghold) formerly stood—
the southern spur of the eastern hill on which
Solomon built his Temple to the north of the old
city. The original exit of this spring was beneath,
and outside, the old city-wall, on the steep side of the
hill, but it was conducted round the hill by a surface-
conduit, and subsequently through a subterranean
tunnel constructed by Hezekiah, to the pool of Siloam
within the city.

Only a little spring, but think what it meant to
Jerusalem. It meant nothing less than *life* to the
city in time of drought and in time of siege. So we
find that the spring is taken by the prophet Isaiah as
typical of the unseen, all-permeating influence of
Jehovah within His city, the source of all spiritual
life and all blessing. We have it so used in Isa.
viii. 6, which speaks of the unfaithful Judæans as
rejecting the waters of Siloam which flow softly, and
as melting for fear before the Syro-Ephraimitish in-
vaders, Rezin and the son of Remaliah.

Now the prophets pictured an ideal Jerusalem as
the heavenly counterpart of the earthly city, and this
they believed was in the future to take the place of
the old Jerusalem. In this glorified city the spring

of Gihon becomes a mighty river, rolling in majesty
down the Kidron valley, and carrying its life-giving
and fertilizing influence wherever it goes. There is
more than one passage in the Old Testament where
this idea comes out. The most important is Ezek.
xlvii., part of the account of Ezekiel's vision of the
ideal Temple of the future on Mount Zion. We
read that the prophet's mysterious guide, the man
with the measuring reed, conducts him to the door of
the Temple, and waters are seen to be issuing from
under the threshold of the Temple eastward. These
at first reach to the ankles; but as the prophet and
his guide advance they quickly increase in volume,
until at last they become " waters of swimming," and
roll in a broad stream down to the Dead Sea, refresh-
ing and fertilizing even that salt and deathly region,
so that trees spring up on the banks, and fishermen
stand and ply their craft. Whether this was pictured
as about to come to pass in actuality we cannot say,
but at any rate the inner meaning is clear. It is the
blessed influence of Jehovah's religion, no longer to
be confined in the future to Jerusalem, but destined
to spread abroad from that centre to the world at
large.

And wherever elsewhere we get this conception of
the river, it is connected with the thought of deliverance and salvation. Thus we read in Isa. xxxiii.[1]—a
prophecy spoken in the midst of the Assyrian crisis
to which we have referred our Psalm—a glowing

[1] Cf. also Joel iii. 18 ; Zech. xiv. 8.

16

description of the ideal Zion of the future, after the passing of the Assyrian peril, and it ends with this wonderful picture : " Look upon Zion, the city of our festal assembly : thine eyes shall see Jerusalem, a quiet habitation, a tent that shall not be removed, the stakes whereof shall never be plucked up, neither shall any of the cords thereof be broken. But there Jehovah will be with us in majesty, a place of broad rivers and streams ; whereon shall go no galley with oars, neither shall gallant ship pass thereby. For Jehovah is our judge, Jehovah is our lawgiver, Jehovah is our king ; He will save us. . . . And the inhabitant shall not say, I am sick : the people that dwell therein shall be forgiven their iniquity." Here is salvation indeed, not merely from the earthly foe, but, what is more vital still, salvation from sin.

So it is that our Psalmist, having mentioned the river, at once connects it with the thought of God's presence in Jerusalem, and His power to save :

" God is in her midst, she shall not be moved ;
God shall help her at the turn of the morning " ;

i.e. at the dawn which will succeed the dark and dreary night.

" Nations roar, kingdoms shake ;
He utters His voice, the earth dissolves.
The Lord of hosts is with us ;
Our stronghold is Jacob's God."

The third stanza, which concludes the Psalm, pictures the total abolition of war in the blessed future—an

ideal to which we too look forward with hope and
longing.

I have spoken at some length already; but before
I stop there is one more thought which I wish to
bring before you as briefly as possible.

The Psalm of which we have been speaking is the
original of the German Luther's well-known hymn,
"Ein' feste Burg ist unser Gott," and is for this
reason so closely associated with his name that it is
often spoken of as "Luther's psalm." No doubt the
Germans are singing this hymn in their churches at
the present time, and applying it in thought to the
crisis at which they, like us, are standing. This
must raise the question in our minds—have we more
right to lay claim to it, to stake our confidence in its
promises, than they have? We believe from the
heart that, as a nation, we *have*. At any rate we
profess the ideals of the old Hebrew religion as
expanded and perfected in Christianity, with its
moral and spiritual requirements; and, broadly speaking, we endeavour as a nation to carry them out.
We have not, as a nation, openly spurned the teaching of Jesus Christ, and adopted the ideal that might
makes right, that the sword must be the final arbiter,
and that success in battle is an end to be attained
through the most callous ruthlessness, the most
fiendish cruelty.

But let us not forget that the nation is but the
aggregate of its individual units, and that on each and

all of these units there lies the solemn duty of making the national profession a reality. It is the lives of every one of us, the standard which we set before us, and the manner in which we live up to it, which go to justify our claim, and which may help, in God's good providence, not merely towards success in the war, but to the best and truest success in the difficult period which lies beyond it.

Let us ask ourselves whether as individuals we are making God our refuge and strength, and relying on Him so to transform our characters and sanctify our lives that we may be worthy of the blessings, temporal and eternal, which He alone is able to bestow.

XX.

OUR LORD'S USE OF THE OLD TESTAMENT.

"The Holy Scriptures, which are able to make thee wise unto salvation, through faith which is in Christ Jesus."—2 TIM. iii. part of 15.

IT is generally admitted, even by those for whom Christianity is but one Religion among many, that no higher standard of living has ever been put forward than that which is exhibited in the life of Jesus Christ. To be as Christ was, the professed and sincere Exponent of the will of the Almighty Being; to live as Christ lived, consciously and continuously framing His life in harmony with this Almighty will —here is an Ideal which, if displayed merely by a man pre-eminently intimate to the Divine mind, must still command the admiration of those who set before themselves the highest development of the human race.

But to us, who, above and beyond this, believe that He—the best and greatest of men—was also very God of very God, one with the Father, in Substance, in Power, and in Eternity, the Organ of God's revealed Will as being the only-begotten Son who is in the

bosom of the Father—to us the human life of such a
One must form the central object for our imitation,
the goal of all our upward striving after God.

We may, therefore, hope to gather much that is
useful for reflection, if we seek to fix our thoughts
upon some special aspect, some single well-defined
practice, of the human life of our Lord, and to consider whether by copy of this we may not advance in
holiness and in likeness to Him. This morning let us
think for a few minutes about the manner in which
our Lord studied and knew the Holy Scriptures, and
the value which these Scriptures possessed for Him as
a man.

1. The fact that Jesus Christ as man had a full and
thorough acquaintance with the Scriptures of the Old
Testament is one which we need not pause to argue.
We know that, in His recorded utterances, He used
them constantly, quoted their words familiarly, and
spoke of them as testifying to Himself. Then comes
the question—a question which is rather apt to be
overlooked, but which may be asked with all reverence
and with great profit to the inquirer—*Whence was this
knowledge derived?* Did it spring necessarily out of
His divine omniscience *as the Son of God*; or was it
the result of the assiduous application of the faculties
of His human mind to reading and study *as a man?*
Here we enter upon a subject which is extremely
difficult and perplexing—the relationship of our
Lord's human knowledge to His divine knowledge.
It is possible, however, to state the problem reverently

and simply; and certainly it is a question which we cannot ignore or neglect if we are to understand the way in which our Lord knew and made use of the Old Testament Scriptures during His earthly life.

The problem is this. We believe that our Lord, as divine—as the Son of God—was omniscient, *i.e.* *all-knowing*, the possessor of infinite knowledge. We cannot, by our own finite understanding, grasp and comprehend all that this means; but we *can* rest assured that there is nothing that God does not know and understand, no fact which He has to acquire by the slow process of study and experience.

On the other hand, we must believe also that our Lord, as the possessor of a perfect human nature, was endowed with *a human mind.* Now it is essentially characteristic of the human mind to be *finite in capacity, i.e.* not to grasp all knowledge in one survey without an effort, but to acquire knowledge bit by bit through learning and everyday-experience.

How can these two forms of knowledge—the divine and the human—have existed side by side in one Person ? How can He, as God, have exercised His faculty of universal knowledge, while, as Man, He exercised the proper human faculty of learning and acquiring knowledge ? We must surely conclude that the two forms of knowledge could not have existed side by side in active exercise. The exercise of the divine faculty of universal knowledge would have done away with the necessity—and even, we may say,

with the *possibility*—of acquiring knowledge through
the ordinary human processes by which men learn
and study. Yet it is of the essence of a perfect
human mind to be finite and limited, to take in
knowledge bit by bit through exercise of the faculties
with which it is endowed by God, and in virtue of the
experiences of everyday-life.

If, therefore, we suppose that our Lord, through
the exercise of His divine faculty of universal knowledge, dispensed with the ordinary processes through
which the human mind is accustomed to acquire
knowledge gradually and laboriously, we are, in fact,
assuming that His Divinity took the place of His
human mind. This is a view which was put forward
in the early days of the Christian Church by a
theologian named Apollinarius ; and it was condemned
by the Church as a misrepresentation of the truth.
It would, as we have seen, make our Lord to be
human merely as regards His *body*, His divine nature
taking the place of a proper human mind : whereas,
on the contrary, the New Testament teaches us that
He took upon Himself *every part* of our human nature
in order that He might uplift it and redeem it, and
of this human nature the reasoning and spiritual part
is the more important. So it is that the Athanasian
Creed speaks of our Lord as " of a reasonable soul and
human flesh subsisting " ; *i.e.* He not only possessed
a human body, but also a *soul* or *mind* which was
reasonable in the sense in which we are accustomed
to apply the term to ourselves—exercised in the

ordinary processes of thought and reasoning which the human mind is accustomed to employ.

How, then, are we to explain the fact that our Lord, possessed as He was of the faculty of divine universal knowledge, was able to bow Himself to the experience of human knowledge? St. Paul, in that great passage in the Epistle to the Philippians, in which he uses our Lord's Incarnation as the supreme example of humility (Phil. ii. 1–11), states that, although He pre-existed in the form of God—*i.e.* in possession of all that is essential to the divine nature—yet He did not regard equality with God as a prize to be clutched at and retained at all hazards, but *emptied Himself*—*i.e.* was content to forego the privileges attaching to Divinity—in order that He might take upon Himself the form—*i.e.*, once more, all the essential characteristics—of a bond-servant, and be found in the likeness of man. And again, in a striking passage in the Second Epistle to the Corinthians (2 Cor. viii. 9), the Apostle uses the words: " Ye know the grace of our Lord Jesus Christ, how that, though He was rich, yet for your sakes *He beggared Himself*, that ye through His poverty might be rich "; *i.e.* not simply that, while here on earth, He lived the life of a poor man, but that He voluntarily surrendered something that is implied in the statement, " though He was rich," namely, some privilege properly attaching to His Divinity. We are justified, therefore, in assuming that this *Self-emptying* or *Self-beggaring* may have included the voluntary surrender, during His earthly life, of the exercise of the faculty of divine knowledge, in order that, so doing, He might subject Himself to the experience of human knowledge in a way which otherwise would have been impossible.

Now, as this is a very vital question for the study of our Lord's Incarnation, and it is most important that we should not go astray and misapprehend the truth, let us test our conclusion by a close parallel— the fact of our Lord's omnipotence, the possession of *all power*, as God, taken in connexion with His constant *habit of prayer* to God the Father during His earthly life.

It is quite certain that, as God of God and of one substance with the Father, all that the Father possessed was also the property of the Son necessarily and by right, because bestowed upon Him from all eternity. Therefore, as God the Son and the Possessor of all things, He needed not to ask anything of the Father, there being no grace, no gift of any kind, by the addition of which He might be enriched. And yet we find Him constantly in the exercise of prayer; spending whole nights in vigil, asking for special privileges to be bestowed upon His Apostles and upon His Church, wrestling in Gethsemane at the supreme crisis of His life.

We must believe, then, that *as Man* He *needed* that experience of communion with God which comes through exercise in prayer, as well as those special gifts and graces which, in answer to prayer, God is willing to bestow.

Thus, in this respect He did not exercise His divine prerogative which might have dispensed with the necessity for prayer, but was content to bow Himself to the completeness of human experience, and not to suffer the omnipotence of His Divinity to obscure the finiteness of His human soul, this finiteness being of the essence of its perfection as human.

Therefore, in the parallel case of His human knowledge, and in that part of it which specially concerns us this morning—His knowledge of the Old Testament Scriptures—we have created an *a priori* supposition (strengthening our former argument) that this knowledge flowed not out of His omniscience as God, but out of the studious application of His human mind, a mind of which the perfection *as human* implied the reception of knowledge, not as a whole, but gradually and part by part. Just as, in the one case, it is clear that He condescended to abjure the privileges of His *omnipotence,* in order that He might undergo the experience of the gaining of grace and help from God the Father through the exercise of prayer; so, in the other case, we may assume that He condescended to abjure the privileges of His *omniscience,* in order that He might share the experience of learning and acquiring knowledge through human channels and by human methods.

Let us now take this supposition of the gradual training and development of our Lord's human mind through study of the Old Testament, and subject it to the test of Gospel-statement. So doing, we find it to be in strict accord with the words of St. Luke, which tell us that "Jesus increased in *wisdom* and stature, and in favour with God and man" (St. Luke ii. 52). We may therefore believe that our blessed Lord read the Scriptures regularly, *i.e.*, no doubt, *daily*, and that He did this for the spiritual benefit of His human soul, and for the instruction of His human mind, as part of the long preparation for His comparatively short ministry in Galilee and Judæa.

He must, indeed, have received wonderful illumination in His studies, through the Holy Spirit which, as St. John tells us, was given unto Him by God "not in measure" (St. John iii. 34). And, without doubt, from His divine Personality there was excluded the very possibility of error, or false interpretation, or misapprehension of the *spiritual* meaning underlying the Law, the Prophets, and the sacred Writings. But as man, and living when and where He did, He would naturally study these books in accordance with the methods and canons of the times, being content to adopt the received views as to their authority and historical value. For while He furnished in Himself a standard of interpretation for all time, He Himself being the goal towards which prophet and psalmist, consciously or unconsciously, strained their rapt gaze and stretched out their eager hands; yet he did not will also to lay down any basis of historical criticism and analysis which should anticipate, limit, or render futile, the results obtained by the future development of critical science.

This was not His purpose. He dealt with the *spiritual truths* contained in the Old Testament—the witness to Himself, the principles of religion and morality—and not with the *framework* wherein these truths lie enshrined. For the spiritual lessons which He was inculcating by reference to the Old Testament stood quite independent of mere questions as to the authorship of its various parts; and any preliminary discussion upon such matters would, at the time, have hindered rather than helped the deep facts of religion which it was His mission to teach.

2. Let us pass on to consider very briefly something of the value which the Scriptures, thus studied, contained for our Lord as Man.

We observe, firstly, that His consciousness of His mission appears to have been derived from them. He constantly speaks of Himself as fulfilling, and that knowingly, the most glowing ideals for the future pictured by the Old Testament writers. He is the *King-Messiah*, the Son of David, Who is to reign over a restored Israel, and Whose Kingdom is to have no end; to Whose light nations are to come, and kings to the brightness of His rising. He is *Jehovah's ideal Servant*, anointed to preach the Gospel to the poor, to be despised, rejected, done to death by His contemporaries, but finally to see of the travail of His soul with satisfaction, the justifier of many as the bearer of their iniquities. He is *Man* in his ideal relation towards God, carrying into effect the Psalmist's words :

> "Then said I, Lo, I am come ;
> In the roll of the book it is written of me :
> I delight to do Thy will, O my God ;
> Yea, Thy law is within my heart" (Ps. xl. 9, 10).

And if, as we must believe, this consciousness had its birth, grew, and came to full development, during those years of preparation for His ministry, what hours of earnest study are here implied!   Often must He have read and re-read those passages which sketched His destiny in lines so bold and realistic ; and often, too, must the prayer have risen to His lips :

> "Shew Thou me the way that I walk in,
> For I lift up my soul unto Thee
>
> .   .   .   .
>
> Teach me to do the thing that pleaseth Thee,
> For Thou art my God ;
> Let Thy loving Spirit lead me forth
> Into the land of righteousness" (Ps. cxliii. 8, 10).

Or again, we see the value of the Scriptures to our blessed Lord in the manner in which He used them to meet the temptations which He had to encounter, whether these rose unbidden to His mind at the direct suggestion of the evil one, or whether they sought to insinuate themselves more indirectly through the hateful craft and enmity of Scribe and Pharisee.   In every case our Saviour was prepared with His answer from the Old Testament Scriptures, "It is written," and in every case He came off victorious, as indeed He could not fail to do.

And lastly, to be brief, it was the Holy Scriptures which formed our Lord's support and consolation at the hour of His death. To them He turned quite naturally to express the deepest need of His human soul :

" My God, my God, why hast Thou forsaken me ? " (Ps. xxii. 1) ;

and probably, as He hung there on the Cross, He repeated to Himself the whole of that xxiind Psalm, with its passionate heart-outpouring and its triumphant conclusion. With the words of another Psalm He yielded up His life :

" Into Thy hands I commend my spirit " (Ps. xxxi. 6),

thereby expressing His voluntary Self-surrender, and His perfect confidence in the committal of His soul to God. And thus—and we may say it with all reverence—these Scriptures of the Old Testament, written by human hands but guided by the Holy Spirit—treasures contained in earthen vessels— formed for our Lord, throughout His human life, a *guide*, a *weapon*, and a *stay*, from first to last.

3. The lesson for ourselves as Christians lies so plainly upon the surface of the subject with which we have been dealing that it scarcely seems to need further pressing home. It is that, if we would seek to imitate the Lord Jesus in His earthly life, we must imitate Him in regular and devotional study of the Bible, as well as in all else wherein He has left us an example that we might follow in His steps.

Bible-study, with earnest desire to gather spiritual good, is just as necessary for our soul's welfare, for its growth in holiness, as is *prayer*: we may hold communion with God in the one as in the other.

As was our Saviour, so are we in this world; and in times of doubt and difficulty, despondency and danger, we shall learn the value of the habit which we have formed, and know indeed that these holy Scriptures are able to make us wise. unto salvation, through faith which is in Christ Jesus.

And as we open the Holy Bible, the peculiar treasure of our Church, let us pray that God the Holy Spirit may dwell richly within us, quickening our earnestness, strengthening our weakness, and guiding us into all truth.

Printed in Great Britain
by Amazon

42105360R00149